# Lilac City Fairy Tales

Published by Cup of Stars Press in 2014

Edited by Sharma Shields
Cover design by Karli Ingersoll
Book design by Keely Honeywell
Printed by Gray Dog Press

# Contents

# Contents continued

# Contents continued

*"In a traditional fairy tale there is no need for a portal. Enchantment is not astounding. Magic is normal."*
—Kate Bernheimer

Sheri Boggs

# FU

The first time I saw her I didn't know what I was seeing. In the park, the moonlight can play tricks on you. Everything is shadows: the pointy evergreens that box in the garden, the dewy carpet of grass, even the brightly regimented flower beds are just dusky hummocks after dark. It was early in summer and the manic glee of running around at night was still new. I couldn't keep up with my older brothers so I collapsed on one of the concrete benches at the end of the garden. And that's when I saw her, or at least glimpses of her among the trees. A generous curve of belly, a glimmering, fathomless eye, a terrible, blubbery mouth. I ran home, not telling anyone what I saw.

I returned the next night. My brothers had recently discovered the joys of mild vandalism -- kicking the heads off marigolds, tearing up clumps of lobelia just to throw at each other. They called it "going to Pete's house," as in hollering out a fake destination as they tumbled out of the house each night. "Take Angus with you," our mom would yell back, even though I kind of wanted to stay. I was the youngest, my two brothers a pair of thick-necked, incurious goons. I watched them race up the hill in football cleats, each wanting to be first to spray-paint bad words onto the side of the greenhouse.

"My brothers are imbeciles," I said, breaking the quiet around me. I waited, listening. Some stars were visible and I opened the "Awesome Astronomy" app on my phone, holding it up to the night sky. The constellations were easy—we covered those in the fourth grade. But sometimes you can see planets, or even the International Space Station on its swift orbit around the earth. The bench was cool under my palms as I craned my neck to peer into the underbrush. Nothing. Whatever was here last night wasn't here any longer. I scuffed a hollow in the gravel with my heel.

"Gimme the paint, spaz."

I sometimes can't tell my brothers' voices apart, but sweat broke out on my forehead as I tried to see across the garden to what they were doing. I wondered if the park employed security guards and how often their rounds were. I closed the app on my phone.

There was a rustling behind me, stealthy enough that it made me hold perfectly still, ears straining. Something was dragging over dry leaves, but I could also make out something like footsteps. I imagined the careful picking up and putting down of giant paws. It got within four feet of where I was sitting, where it was still hidden by cedar branches and then sort of hunkered down. I stayed frozen, silently telling my heart to stop beating so freaking loud.

I made out a sort of muzzle, a broad nose with wide nostrils, a sorrowful face. Its crazy mouth was open with its tongue hanging out, flanked by some capable-looking incisors. It reminded me of one of my mom's bookends, or the statues outside Chinatown in Portland. "They're Fu Dogs," she'd explained. "They're sort of a lion dog. They bring prosperity, or good luck." She added, seeing the blank look on my face. She told me about how they come in pairs, and that the boy Fu Dog rests his paw on a globe and the girl Fu Dog rests her paw on a baby. At the time my mom seemed happy and I couldn't imagine us needing prosperity. But now, my dad gone and my mom so tired, a little prosperity might do us good.

"H- hey there... fella. Um, where's your globe?" I asked. My brothers had vanished, off to break into the park's cafe or lop the heads off rose bushes, but I knew I couldn't be too careful.

The creature swung its head around to stare at me. I jumped—the movement so sudden and unexpected. "Whoa, easy," I said. It gave me a disdainful look, then shifted onto its haunches and rolled to one side. Even in the dark I could make out teats. Whatever it was, it wasn't a boy.

We sat there in the silence for a moment. I turned the astronomy app on my phone back on and offered her the screen. My sudden, numb-skulled gesture scared her and she withdrew into the shadows. I set the phone down, holding my hands up to indicate I was harmless. "It's ok," I said. "I won't hurt you." She slowly came forward, her nostrils flared and twitching.

"That's Cassiopeia, from Greek mythology" I said, thrilling when she followed my pointed finger to gaze up at the "W" in the night sky. "And that's Draco," I said. I pointed out all the constellations I could remember, even making up a few. I couldn't believe most of her head had emerged from the brush. "I'm sure you know the Big Dipper and the Little Dipper," I allowed. "That's the Even Littler Dipper," I said, pointing out a tiny cluster of stars. Our first joke. It could have been a trick of my peripheral vision but I could swear her lip curled up in a smile.

And from that night on, we fell into a pattern. At first I followed my miscreant brothers. By the end of summer I was sneaking out. A couple of times I brought food—a plate of leftovers, a bag of jerky, a box of Red Vines from going to a movie. She never ate in front of me, but I'd find the empty plate or wrappers on my next visit. I talked to her about anything I could think of, at first telling her stuff I thought she should know—the Latin names of the trees in the park, how electricity works, which houses in the neighborhood had guns. Gradually I told her other things, about how lame my brothers were, about my mom, my dad. I liked seeing her big inscrutable eyes turned in my direction. She was always panting, her breath terrible but sort of comforting. One time she brought me a strip of raw meat, leaving it on a maple leaf so I could eat it after she departed. I couldn't bring myself to eat it raw but I cooked it at home that night, its gamey smell permeating the kitchen after my mom had gone to bed.

I wanted to ask her what she was, but I didn't want to offend her. I'd been looking her up for weeks, digging out my dad's old encyclopedias in the basement, reading about mythical creatures on wikipedia. I even took a bus up to the library and spent an afternoon reading about cryptids. From my research, the closest I got was that she was sort of like a fu dog, sort of like a Japanese guard dog called a nekomata, sort of like a manticore, maybe even a little bit like a griffin. She didn't have wings—that much I could tell. But even as weeks became months, she stayed in the shadows.

When I went home each night, thoughts of her followed me into sleep. I dreamed about sleeping on a bed of pine needles, of curling up next to her massive flank. Sometimes I even dreamed of our bodies merging together, becoming a dreadful and roaring uber-beast. The night before my old life ended, I dreamed of chasing down and eating a deer.

The smell of forest fires and burning grass signaled the coming end of summer. I had no wish to return to nights doing homework and days dodging bullies. School would start in a week and my brothers had grown bored with throwing beer bottles in the duck pond, weary of chasing geese and toilet papering the gardens. They looked toward me for their last taunting.

"Why do you just sit here all the time," one asked.

"Yeah," accused the other. He horked a wad of cloudy spit out the side of his mouth.

I shrugged. My beast friend wasn't here yet. I hoped they'd go away soon.

"You sound like a 'tard. You know that right? Just sitting here talking to yourself? Does mom know you just sit here talking to yourself?"

There was the softest sound coming from the trees behind me, the pressure of foot pads settling onto dirt and duff. I wondered if my brothers could hear it.

One brother had his knife out, this ridiculous contraption from the hunting store in town, with a five-inch serrated blade and some other "tools" tucked away in its recesses. He especially liked the bottle opener, but even more than that he just liked to clean his fingernails with the big blade.

"You haven't done shit this summer," the oldest pointed out. "You need to get your hands dirty at least once."

"Yeah," said the other. He was a real brainiac, that one. A thought flickered across his normally dim face. "Hey, we should go fuck up the fish pond. Angus has to catch a fish with his bare hands before we let him go home." In the shadow of the tree I heard a soft, but angry, chuff.

My oldest brother giggled. He scraped away at the tree trunk with his knife. I watched as he started to carve a letter in the tree trunk. "F". Of course. "Fuck" was such an imaginative word to carve into things. He paused before starting on the "U."

"Hey, I've got one better," he said. "He has to kill it before we let him go home. He has to actually step on its motherfucking head and crush it." He chortled to himself as he finished the upcurve of the U. "Grab his hands," he suddenly said. "We're gonna make him do this." As my younger brother lunged for me I heard a thunderous reaction from under the tree.

"Shit!" yelled my oldest brother, stepping back. My creature—my manticore, my nekomata, my fu dog—emerged from the brush. She was gigantic and beautiful: her teeth bared and her eyes wild and rolling with rage. I stared, awestruck. She opened her terrible mouth and roared—a ghastly, unearthly sound. The brother with the knife went for her with it. She took him out with a swift and merciless paw, his bones crushing with the impact as his body landed in the trees about fifty feet away. The other brother started to run and she lunged after him, as fluid and terrifying as a Chinese dragon. She scooped him up with her jaws and tossed him in the air before swallowing him whole. She was magnificent.

She turned to me then, I cleaned her bloodied muzzle with my T-shirt. She rubbed her massive head against me as I worked, and I stared at her monstrous, powerful body. She smelled like the forest.

My old life was over. My life with the beast began.

Shann Ray

# Archangel

*—for Andrew Wolf*

### 1.
His rage
started as less than an itch
but before long he found
himself caught in
ridiculous contortions just
to dig his nails into the lump
on his back.

### 2.
The compulsion made him
hurt himself,
gravely,
as if for years
some alternate spike
or knot of bones
was forming

### 3.
beneath the surface of his shoulder blades.
He practiced accomplishing
just the right dislocation
of socket, radius, elbow, and wrist
in order to rake at what
festered, no,
gestated there, symmetrical, bisected

4.
by the column
of his spine.  Over and again
he opened
the skin, bloodied his hands,
knuckle and print, crease and lifeline
to find what bloomed in him
was not infection, not fever

5.
but wings.
Great wings unfolding up out
the reverse side
of his ribcage.
Out of his own
good body
his aeronautic devices rose

6.
taller than a man.
Primary feathers on hardy
grey quills longer
than the swords
of kings.
Secondary feathers
and flight feathers

7.
myriad in their
bright containment.
He closed his eyes, feeling
them arch high above his head, robe his frame
and drape the floor behind him.  And when
he opened his eyes, what he saw he named
forgiveness.

Simeon Mills

# Fourth Grade

Our bus driver was a robot. Ask any kid on the bus. Not that any of them knew what a robot looked like. But once Mrs. Stover showed up behind the wheel all our fellow bus riders were suddenly robotical engineers from MIT. Fine. I guess they weren't complete novices. They had all seen *Star Wars* at least, or randomly flipped through the "R" volume of *Encyclopedia Britannica*, or overheard their parents curse all the new technology taking over the world. But had they ever seen a *real* robot before our bus driver? (Well. That they recognized, anyway.) I'll clarify: Mrs. Stover was a robot, but, unlike my brother and me, there was a mountain of evidence condemning her.

"She doesn't eat. Not even the day after Halloween when I gave her a Twix just to see if she'd eat it. She didn't."

"Mrs. Stover drinks too much coffee, just like a robot."

"And her hair. It's wires. It just sits up there."

"I heard robots eat cigarettes. Her breath smells like my grandma."

"Her glasses are too big for a human."

"Has anyone ever seen her *out* of her bus seat? Because it's like— . . . it's like she's *connected* to the bus, like they're two parts of the same big— . . . *machine*."

"And Magic Johnson."

"Magic Johnson."

"I was about to say, *Magic Johnson*."

It was true. Mrs. Stover had a computer-like obsession with Magic Johnson. All of her clothes were Lakers purple. (One poor kid even saw a flash of purple underwear once.) She had pictures of Magic Johnson on her steering wheel. Lakers earrings. Lakers fingernail polish. Lakers thermos. Mrs. Stover had a price of admission to board her bus: tell her a fact about Magic Johnson. Some kids gave the same answer every day: "He wears purple." That was enough. These kids could sit wherever they wanted. But if you were a new kid? If you stepped into her bus and knew *nothing* about Magic Johnson? You had to sit directly behind Mrs. Stover for the duration of the ride. You had to listen. Correct that: the *entire bus* had to listen to Mrs. Stover's booming voice, re-announcing highlights from the previous night's Lakers game or, if it was the off-season, endless trivia about Magic Johnson in frantic, high-pitched shouts: "THREE-TIME NBA CHAMPION . . ." A short pause. "FINALS MVP HIS ROOKIE SEAON . . ." Kids held their breath. "SIX-FOOT-NINE . . ."

James Conroy had been first to realize she was a robot. Surprisingly, it had nothing to do with Magic Johnson. Instead James pointed out the writing on the backs of Mrs. Stover's shoes. It was in a foreign language—an entirely foreign alphabet. We all snuck peeks to the front of the bus, where Mrs. Stover's shoes worked the pedals. There was the writing, easy to confirm, yet impossible to explain: 会談する. Nobody could even begin to sound these words out. "Robots are built on the other side of the earth," James whispered. "In China."

Everyone gasped: *China.*

That discovery occurred the first week of fourth grade. By Spring *Mrs. Stover is a robot* had yet to be replaced by anything even half as interesting to talk about on our bus. New theories and observations sprang up daily to be debated, scrutinized and—if validated by James Conroy, the official robot expert on the bus—formally recorded in Molly Reed's spiral notebook. Molly sat with James in the back of the bus. She was his second-in-command, his vice-president and secretary, all in one. Molly's notebook contained every scrap of evidence against Mrs. Stover, page after page, written in flawless handwriting, even by girl-standards. She guarded the notebook with her life; James was the only other person permitted to hold it. To Molly, the rumor about Mrs. Stover went beyond gossip. There was an inevitable conclusion, a purpose to her methodical data collection: on the last day of school she and James would submit their findings to the principal, and Mrs. Stover would be destroyed. *This is serious you guys*, she whispered whenever the conversation got too silly or fun. She was heartless. A professional. Her tiny glasses, tiny nose and general overall smallness only added to the effect. Molly Reed hated Mrs. Stover because Mrs. Stover was a robot. For whatever reason, my twin brother, Kanga, was in love with Molly Reed.

Fourth grade was a do-or-die year for robots of our make and model. It's when our parents became obsolete and vanished. One morning they were here, moving about our closet in routine fashion, watching TV, drinking coffee, getting me and Kanga ready for the bus, etc. When we got home from school they were gone. Mom and Dad's possessions remained, each in its respective corner of the closet, and, for better or for worse, the smell of Mom and Dad remained too, even if their nut and bolt bodies were somewhere . . . else.

Kanga and I had competing theories as to *how* and *why* our parents left. I told my brother that our parents' brains contained a dormant program on a 10-year timer; when the timer went off, Mom and Dad stopped whatever they were doing, walked to the bus stop and traveled to their new home, probably a laboratory somewhere. Or maybe they walked straight to the dump and—

"Don't say that!" Kanga plugs his ears with his thumbs. "Mom and Dad aren't in a dump. And they would never just leave us like that. Somebody— " We were standing in the closet, suddenly huge without Mom and Dad in it. Kanga spun around, checking each corner as if Mom and Dad might still be there. They weren't. "Somebody must've kidnapped them. Somebody's got them in their basement all chained up. We gotta save them!"

With our mouths shut, Kanga and I were identical twin brothers. Mom could tell us apart by looking at us, but nobody else could, not even Dad. We had our differences though. Not to put too fine a point on it: I was the good robot, and Kanga was . . . Well. While *I* fully understood that our purpose as robots was to covertly navigate our environment, to interact with our human peers *just enough* to appear normal, to speak sentences to them (but only after having listened to 100 sentences spoken *by* them), and, above all else, TO AVOID DETECTION, Kanga felt our purpose was to simply be human.

"Look around," I told him. "Do you see any signs of a struggle here? Mom and Dad weren't kidnapped. They left on their own. They—" I had to choose my words carefully with Kanga. "It wasn't up to them, okay? Mom and Dad only did what they were pro-gramed to do. They didn't want to leave. They had no choice about it. I'm sure they— . . . I'm sure they still *love* us, wherever they are."

Kanga crossed his arms. He closed his eyes. "Somebody shot them in the head."

"Look." My patience was gone. "We both knew this was coming. The whole procedure is spelled out very clearly in The Directions, page 593. Do I need to reread that section to you?"

"No."

"Because I can. The Directions are right over—"

"Don't." Kanga opened his eyes. "Please."

"Okay." I was playing dirty. If Mom had ever needed to get Kan-ga to shape up, she just threatened to read The Directions to him. I'll admit, The Directions was a spectacularly eye-glazing bore of a book, but that wasn't why Kanga hated it. The Directions was a how-to guide for being a robot—specifically, for being *us*, a pair of male Detroit 600's (and our parent units). I read it to understand my strengths and weaknesses as a robot. Kanga avoided it for exactly the same reason.

But even my brother could see that Mom and Dad were inferior to us. Don't get me wrong. I loved them, but facts are facts. Our par-ents were built for a single purpose: to see Kanga and myself safely through our early years—and not a moment longer. Mom and Dad did an admirable job. We survived. Dad didn't run us over with a lawn mower (though he once trimmed the toe of Kanga's sneaker). And Mom read us bedtime stories every night. But should a three-year-old have to correct his mother on the word "caboose"?

I was ready for Mom and Dad to hit the road by second grade. I had learned everything I could from them (not much) and by then they were just getting in the way. Mom always made us stand in a circle together for dinner, which was pointless, because robots don't eat. And she only had one question she was programmed to ask: "How was school, honey?"

"Well," I'd respond, "it was an interesting day, Mom. Last night the school got infested with giant flesh-eating moles. They killed our custodian. The principal told each kid to bring a knife to school to-morrow for protection. Or swords, if we have any."

Mom would just smile and nod. "That's nice, honey."

So I'd turn to Dad. "Do we have any swords, Dad? For school? Really sharp ones?"

Dad would take a long drink of beer. He'd clear his throat. "Ask your mother."

Standing beside me, Kanga would give me a kick to the shin . . .

It's sad, I guess. Their central processors weren't advanced enough to handle the data speeds required for quality human interaction. They didn't leave the closet, except on outings programmed into their tiny list of dialog options. The gas station, the liquor store, the library—even those exchanges were embarrassing to witness. The duck pond at the park. Mom used to go there with a loaf of bread and leave us in the car while she fed the ducks.

If you asked Kanga what was so great about them, he'd probably say standing between them and watching TV. Mom on one side, Dad on the other, their hips bonking against his shoulders like he was a toy. That made Kanga laugh and laugh and laugh. I'd be on top of the washing machine (that was my spot) trying to watch in peace until I'd give up and do my homework.

Mom got it into Kanga's head that we were all some kind of "family," but The Directions included just one chapter on how to fix Mom and Dad. The other 3,000+ pages were about maintenance for me and Kanga. Our bodies were designed to evolve over time, to grow, to age. Nothing about our parents ever changed.

The day they disappeared was the best of my life.

But then I had to step up and became a second mom to Kanga. Not *our* mom, but a late model version of her that saw right through his BS. After our parents left, or died, or whatever happened to them, Kanga fell into odd behavior. It's Robots 101 to *never* put food directly into your mouth, much less swallow any (unless equipped with a food receptacle). I mastered that rule as an infant. But two days after our parents' disappearance, as we boarded Mrs. Stover's bus, instead of asking us a trivia question like usual she held out a basket of candy and said, "TRIPLE DOUBLE LAST NIGHT." It was nearly the end of the school year, and by now we knew a triple double meant Magic Johnson had tallied at least 10 points, 10 rebounds and 10 assists. We politely accepted our food and stuffed it in our pockets for "later". That's what *I* did. Kanga unwrapped his and placed it in his mouth. "T'ank 'ou," he rasped as the watermelon cube plugged his chest valve. I escorted him to our seat: Kanga by the window, me on the aisle. I was so disgusted I could hardly look at him—my brother casually trying to stick his whole hand down his throat to retrieve the candy. He couldn't. It was stuck there until lunch recess, when I pulled him behind a garbage dumpster and jimmied the candy out with a ruler. The thing was eight and a half inches down in there. Idiot.

Not that my own behavior was beyond criticism. It was our "birthday" a couple weeks after Mom and Dad left. The Directions spelled out exactly how independent adolescent robots could apply for their birthday gifts, which should cost no more than $25. I filled out the form and mailed it to the address in Detroit, and the day before our birthday one Magic Johnson uniform arrived, shipped to "Darryl and Kanga Livery." The uniform cost $50. I explained on the form that Kanga and I would *share* it, when, really, I had no such intention. I wore the Magic uniform to school for the rest of fourth grade. As far as I could tell, Kanga didn't even know what color a basketball was . . .

Summer couldn't get here fast enough. Keeping Kanga in check at school was giving me premature zits. I had to practically sit on his lap in Mrs. Bingus's room (we had the same teacher), just to make sure he didn't swallow his art project or mention our parents had abandoned us. He was always pretending to cry for no reason. We were lucky Mrs. Bingus was neck deep her own divorce and had been too distracted to send Kanga to the school counselor. Not that I could ever relax. Not even on the bus. Kanga's obsession with Molly Reed had worsened. He stared at her constantly, and the other kids had begun to notice.

On the morning of the last day of school, Kanga pressed his forehead to the bus window as we stopped in front of Molly's filthy gray house. Nobody had mown the lawn all spring. There was a truck parked sideways in her driveway. And where was Molly? Mrs. Stover honked. She honked again, and finally started to move . . . then Molly sleepily emerged from her house, leaving her front door open, so Kanga could get a peek into her living room: a white wall, bare. Molly hugged her notebook to her chest as she walked down the aisle. By now it was filled with so much evidence that an extra 40 pages had been stapled to the back cover.

Today was the big day. If they didn't chicken out, Molly and James would be submitting the notebook to the authorities by first bell. I imagined Principal Vanderlaan's glasses popping off his face as he read the hundreds of damning facts proving our bus driver was a robot. None of us—certainly not I—seemed to care that Molly's actions would result in Mrs. Stover being scrapped or, at best, sold to China to clean windows on skyscrapers. If Mrs. Stover was a faulty robot, so be it. Excitement over her impending demise had diverted attention away from Kanga's weirdness. Once summer arrived, I'd have time to read The Directions in depth and recalibrate his central processor for optimal performance in fifth grade. I seemed to recall a procedure for erasing a robot's memory. Kanga just needed to survive one more day of school.

Molly wasn't making it easy for him. While she had appeared exhausted just moments before, Molly became euphoric when she sat next to James. She couldn't sit still. She couldn't lower her voice. The notebook was open as she read passages aloud, giggling and breathing heavily. When Mrs. Stover halted the bus at the railroad tracks, Molly stood up on her seat and hollered: "Yo! Robot!"

Mrs. Stover slowly turned and faced us. "I'LL BE HAPPY TO TAKE MY FOOT OFF THE BRAKE, YOUNG LADY, WHEN YOUR BUTT IS WHERE I WANT IT."

Molly plopped down, but not without hooting, "Okay, *robot!*"

James was anxious now. He touched Molly's shoulder, to calm her, but she just flapped her arms, notebook and all, sending pages scattering over the back of the bus. I didn't remember moving, but my own hand was now resting on Kanga's shoulder. His muscles hummed with jealousy as he watched James rubbing Molly's back. Whatever James was doing appeared to be working. Molly looked sleepy again. She tipped toward James, sniffing his shirt collar.

"Kanga," I said. "How about after school we go catch some frogs in Culver's Creek. You can flush one down the toilet." Kanga always asked if we could do this, and I always said *No*, because that's what Mom always said. But it was liberating, now, to simply suggest Kanga do exactly what he wanted. Because why not? Because maybe *that* was part of being a mom too: giving your kid that stupid, special thing that only he wanted. And Kanga needed something to distract him. "And maybe we'll chop down that pine tree behind the apartment building too. You know, the one you think looks like a crocodile standing on his—"

"She's whispering to him."

It was true. Molly's lips were practically inside James's ear. It made the hair on the back of my neck itch, just watching her. I wondered if Molly was planning on giving up the notebook operation. She was passionate, whatever she was whispering. James looked terrified. "Ignore her," I said to Kanga. "You have to. Because it's obvious she likes James, but they'll probably break up over the summer. Just wait your turn. Next year, you know? Next year we'll sit closer to Molly on the bus, and—"

"But what's she saying to him? She doesn't look right. I'm going to—"

"Kanga—"

Kanga was crawling over our seat-back (I had a grip on his left arm) when James screamed. After that, nobody moved. The bus just watched in horror.

Turns out there *is* a program to delete memories. I ran it on Kanga that summer, and we got mixed results. Mom and Dad? Mostly history. That time I threw a croquet mallet and it cracked Kanga in the ribs? Gone. But some memories, we learned, are too ingrained to be successfully erased. They aren't stored in a robot's central processor, but somewhere else. The hair on the back of your neck, for instance. The point of your chin. The surface of your eyeballs. Molly Reed going berserk on James was one such memory.

It started with her coughing. But not a normal cough. Molly's cough was like a vacuum cleaner sucking dirt off the bus floor. James tried to push her away, but Molly only fell against him harder. Her eyes bulged—they had become purple—as she glared into James's mouth. James screamed again, and that's when Molly stuck a finger in her own mouth, the way someone might try to find a hair they accidentally ate. What Molly located instead was a gray electrical wire hiding on the back of her tongue. She began yanking it out. The electrical wire fell on James's lap, foot after foot, until Molly at last regurgitated a small silver battery. The writing on the battery was in Chinese, but I recognized the shape and style of it from a catalog Dad had hidden in the closet. This type of battery was used to power Molly's respiration unit. It was the same battery Kanga and I used.

How long did this episode take? 18 seconds. 19 seconds, tops. Molly clawing open her neck took much longer. For some reason, her chewed-up fingernails simply could not puncture the synthetic skin protecting her neck. When they finally did—when that mess of wires, tubing and red lubricating oil spilled onto James's clean white shirt—it was clear to the entire bus *exactly* what Molly Reed was.

Except for Mrs. Stover. She kept driving.

Kanga tried to break free of my grasp, to rescue Molly from what would happen next, but in the history of the world, no kid has ever broken free from his mother to chase a bouncing ball into oncoming traffic. I nearly broke my brother's arm, but Kanga stayed in our seat. I wrapped by hand over his mouth, just to be extra safe.

It was the day before summer. Outside, blue skies. A warm breeze. Our bus windows were open. Upon gathering his wits, James took hold of Molly's thin body and angled her head-first through his window. We didn't hear Molly strike the asphalt, just the rattle of the bus continuing down the road, toward school. Nobody said a word, but a moment later the brakes hissed.

We heard the gentle *beep . . . beep . . . beep* of the bus reversing.

Parked on the side of the road, Mrs. Stover painfully got out of her seat. She never even glanced at us, just walked down her steps and around the bus to inspect the wreckage of our robotic classmate. Half of Molly was on the road, half of her in the gravel. Mrs. Stover lit a cigarette. She took two puffs, chuckled to herself, and bit the cigarette between her teeth. She bent down, grabbed Molly's ankle, and dragged her completely off the road. Mrs. Stover opened the rear door of the bus and took out an orange cone. She tossed it toward Molly. She took another drag on her cigarette, threw it in the dirt and stepped on it, then re-boarded the bus.

On the way to school (we weren't even late) we listened as Mrs. Stover used the radio: "GOTTA CODE EIGHTEEN. CORNER OF ROWELY ROAD AND DIETZ." Short pause . . . "TEN-FOUR."

I tried to let go of him. I did. But my fingers were magnetized to the wiring in Kanga's left arm. My magnets had been switched on by the excitement, I guess, and there was nothing I could do to turn them off. We were conjoined, whether Kanga liked it or not, as we de-boarded the bus, and my fingers had him locked up for the rest of fourth grade. All in all, my brother impressed me that day. He didn't cry. He didn't act up. He just shut himself down and let me drag him wherever we needed to go.

That afternoon, as she dropped us off in front of our apartment building, Mrs. Stover aimed her thick glasses at me and said, "SAY HI TO YOUR MOM FOR ME."

"You bet," I smiled. "Have a great summer, Mrs. Stover. Go Lakers!"

Kanga and I watched Mrs. Stover drive off. "Let go of me now," he whispered. "Please."

I was finally able to release him, so I did. But before he could run away I gave my twin brother a huge hug.

"What's wrong with you?" he said, squirming away from me.

"Nothing." I squeezed harder. "You're a good kid, Kanga." My skin was tingling with a new feeling, a *parental* feeling, half-horror/half-relief, of having witnessed someone *else's* kid make an irreparable mistake, one your own kid could learn from. The Molly Reed experience made us stronger. "If you do everything I say, Kanga, nobody will ever hurt you. Got that?"

"Fine," he said. "But what if the Incredible Hulk jumps down from that tree and tries to kill me?"

"I'll rip him apart with my bare hands."

Kanga laughed, but I cracked my knuckles, and I knew my mom-strength could kill the Incredible Hulk if it had to.

Tim Greenup

# The Couple Speaks of Magic

Sharma says that magic is normal
and Sam says Magic is anything but.
Could a normal person handle the ball like that?
Could a normal person get HIV

and shock the world like that?
He pulls a book from the shelf and chucks it
through the wall and into the neighbor's garage.
Well, could a normal person do such things?

He crumbles to the ground, crying.
Let me think about it, Sharma says.
She takes a drink.
Imagines a world without feet.

A world where *corn* can stand only for something delicious
and sweet. I think a normal person could, she says.
Oh, how we have lost our way, Sam screams
and bursts into green flame.

The children rise from their beds.
They're wearing their paper sleeping gowns.
They huddle around Sam's burning body
and whisper Magic's name.

# We Need to Talk

Terry and I need a break.
We drive west for days.
An Agricultural Inspector at the
state line pulls us aside.

you nebraska boys
ain't smugglin'
no despair into this state
of california, is ya?

Both thumbs tucked
firmly between the straps
of his yellowed overalls, his
immense pinked and pimpled
forehead furrows and sweats.

no sir! our voices suddenly
emphatic and in perfect harmony.

wellll, go 'head on, then.

He nods toward the sun
and grins; he's handsome
beyond belief.

me and my men will
be taking your car, though.

so it goes! says Terry. And
throws him the keys.

Our calves convulse
and skip through a turnstile
into the desert.

We reach the coast
and stop skipping.
In a gasp between
laughters, a beeping
from my pocket.

oh! I say. my phone! almost forgot!
a message! from...julie...she says
we need to talk.

A series of scarlet
flashes. The palms
become ash. Every
beached body burns.

# The Backyard Song

Out here in the fields
we're always orbiting.
I orbit my wife, which
is all right, usually.

At the barbecue I orbit
the grill, while Dan tells jokes
and my wife laughs.

Since when have they been sleeping
together? The acid strip
pressed against my cheek

floods me with Spiritus Mundi
and computers lining
the walls flash:
           warning! warning!
           contaminant detected!

Back in the tool shed
Dan tells me presences
holler from his bookshelf
and frighten his children,
their brains' many colored wires.

That makes me uneasy,
so we examine the hedge
trimmers for hours

into the darkest night
we have ever seen.

# The Father

Your eyes itch. They're tired
of being sprayed with metal shavings.
You find a melon baller. Run its edge over a flame.

First, compression. Then, an undoing.
A dripping down your nose and face.
World swells and you

wake the next weekend in a bloody bed.
Your wife is dead. A deaf toddler
keeps crying from some distant doorway.
Its corduroyed legs quiver. It signs – milk! milk! –
tiny fist pulsing.

Years ago you waded through
cornfields with a wrench. You'd climb onto giant sprinklers
twelve hours a day. The sun dared your skin
not to red, and your skin grew a furry suit.

But how, now, can a bear assuage
this child's emptiness and fear?
When you rise, the child runs
down the hall, trips over its child feet,
slams its head through a wall,
looks back with child eyes and blames you.

# My Week

Monday an envelope arrived
with a red mustache inside

I set it aside and busied myself
with other things

Later a box of bones
showed up on my stoop

Nothing happened for a few days
I drove to work and back

listening to Van Morrison
like I always do

Saturday a green van
hand delivered a plastic bag –

blood and freckled skin
Next morning the clanging

of pots and pans woke me
Downstairs James Joyce

was cooking corned beef
Hello he said and kissed me

I fell into the oven
and he shoved his face

between my legs
I pulled him toward the coals

and made him pray
we never be forgiven

Sharma Shields

# The Frog Prince

Every now and then, a frog becomes what you need.

I kiss a frog in Colorado and he turns into a golden retriever, a frog in Panama becomes a La-Z-Boy recliner. When winter comes I travel the world: a frog in Battle Creek transforms into a blue cashmere scarf, in the Odaesan Mountains a Korean water toad changes into a cinnamon roll. As a solitary princess, you learn to be grateful for any small gift.

In January I kissed a frog in Antwerp, Belgium and she turned into a ferocious old schoolmarm. The schoolmarm knocked me on the head with her umbrella and called me a pervert, and she's been traveling with me ever since.

When we return home to the Northwest, the schoolmarm presents me with a photo album. I'm glad I kissed that poison dart frog in Rurrenabaque; my lips swelled up for a week, but he turned into a digital camera. In the pictures, I stand in front of castles and ruins around the world, my crown lopsided on my head, my gown looking hot and scratchy and out-of-place. It makes me happy to be home again, sitting comfortably in my La-Z-Boy recliner, waiting for sundown.

It's spring here, mating season for the frogs, but when I go to them, it's not romantic or tender.

I crawl through the mud on my hands and knees and unearth a Western Chorus frog. His eyes bulge as I draw him near. I close my eyes and kiss him flat on his lipless mouth. He changes swiftly, this time into a preschooler, plump and naked except for the crown on his head.

The schoolmarm rings the dinner bell. I take up the child's hand. The golden retriever meets us at the drawbridge, tail wagging.

The frogs, undisturbed now, begin to sing. Some nights they sing about their anger, other nights about hunger or loneliness. Tonight, it's a different tune. The child hears it, too. He lifts his smiling face to me, "They're happy."

"They're tired," I say, and the truth is that the one does not cancel out the other.

# The Evil Queen Goes Mirror Shopping

The shopkeeper can sense a big sale pending: the customer is richly dressed, keen-eyed, examining every mirror in sight. She is determined to choose *something*. The shopkeeper is no fool: he knows how to capitalize on desire.

"These," he says to her, waving a hand around the display area, "are pedestrian mirrors. Trinkets, really. I can tell you're a discerning customer. Let me show you our treasures."

She looks right at him – into him, he feels – and he is cut by the obsidian sharpness of her beauty.

*This is no ordinary aristocrat*, the shopkeeper thinks, but he is not easily intimidated, not by her wealth or good looks and not by the bodyguards flanking the shop's doors. He guides her confidently into a backroom and sweeps away a velvet cover from the largest of the displayed mirrors.

"Forged in the Black Caves by dwarves," he says. "This mirror will never tell a lie."

The woman runs her hands along the gleaming frame. She studies herself in the mirror carefully, turning first one way, then another. She unfolds with a bored sigh.

Her glance falls on the far wall. She points to an oval mirror with a large wooden frame.

"Oh," the shopkeeper laughs, "that one is a recent return. His last owner called him a brownnoser. He caused some serious mischief. We're planning to destroy it today."

The customer stands before the mirror and leans in, interviewing it. The mirror answers her in a low, ponderous tone. She rises, satisfied, and snaps her fingers. A guard approaches with a sack of gold.

The shopkeeper hesitates, vaguely sensing what will happen as a result of the sale: a girl's lonely childhood, an attempted murder, a poisoned apple, the long, boring sequester in a glass coffin. But the money is heavy and warm in his hands and he thinks of another little girl, his niece, and how she's never had anything fancy to wear. Her birthday, he remembers, is next week.

"The customer is always right," the shopkeeper says, and bows.

The mirror chuckles its approval.

# Sibling Rivalry

Later, it becomes a competition: who was braver, Hansel or Gretel?

Gretel argues that she was braver. After all, who shoved the witch into the oven?

Hansel argues that he was braver. Who held Gretel's hand in the forest when she whimpered and sobbed for their father? Who whispered to her to stay strong while he, preparing to be devoured, crouched in the witch's cage?

Gretel rolls her eyes. Whose dumbshit idea were the breadcrumbs?

Hansel fumes. Who, at least, had ideas?

But the next day when their families prepare to leave Disneyland, all of their children packed into the cars, the spouses looking weary after a week of sun and souvenirs, Hansel and Gretel embrace, because who else understands?

Then they release one another and depart for their own safe homes, where they each care for their children in a way no adult cared for them.

Rachel Toor

# The Work

No one ever asked why she wanted them. No one ever thought about what she did with them, why she was willing to pay for something most people would just as soon throw out. At first she got away with leaving only a nickel. Now, especially in cities like New York and Los Angeles, the going rate could be as high as five bucks. No, they didn't think about her at all, just focused on the transaction.

As long as the little fuckers wiggled and worried them loose, tongued and fingered them when they become wobbly, as long as once they'd fallen out the spoiled brats placed them under their pillows, Lois was happy to collect, no questions asked.

She didn't pay much attention, just swooped in, all in a night's work. But then this one kid wrapped an upper incisor in blue tissue paper, tied it with a bow, and put it in a baggie. Lois thought, "Fussy," as she left a dollar in its place.

The next time, a molar was wrapped and bagged but next to it Lois also found a peppermint candy. Why was this kid sleeping with candy under her pillow? WTF? Lois took the tooth but left the candy and a buck.

Months later the same kid put a Reese's Peanut Butter Cup in the baggie with the tooth. The kid was doing some kind of reverse Trick or Treating. Clearly no one had explained things to her, including the propensity of chocolate to melt.

It went on like this for years. The kid's baggies always contained a tooth and something else: a sock monkey, a cherry pie, a box of paper clips, a steaming double espresso, dreams, a grandfather clock. Lois took them all, left a dollar, and thought the kid needed help.

Then this kid, who was always reading, always looking things up on the interwebz, always asking her parents questions they couldn't answer, started poking around. Who, she wondered, would pay for discarded body parts? She posted on chat forums and considered different theories: the teeth were bought by a coalition of old people who had lost theirs. The teeth were sold for disturbingly life-like children's dolls. The teeth had hallucinogenic properties when ground up and snorted. Why would anyone want them? They had to have some value.

One night, there was only a tooth and a note. It said,

Dear Tooth Fairy,

I try not to be creeped out that you come into my private space when I'm sleeping and root around under my pillow. I know about stranger danger and kiddie fiddlers but I don't want to let my parent's paranoia keep me from leading a rich and full life. Because you're purchasing my teeth, I trust you have some use for them. Can you tell me please what you do with them?

Your friend.

Lois thought, *The nerve!* Lois thought, *Kiddie fiddlers?* Lois thought, *No one has ever asked before.*

For so long she'd been on her own. She'd sacrificed sleep and meaningful social contact in order to gather her materials. She'd nearly blown through the coin left to her by her parents. She lived in the corner of her hovel so she'd have enough studio space to work. She took only what others no longer needed and remunerated them, she thought, handsomely. She had only her imagination, her drive, her need to create.

Lois looked at the piece. There were parts she liked, and parts she knew just didn't work. Sometimes she thought it was brilliant, and other times she wanted to lay waste to the whole project. Sections had been built and rebuilt, crafted and revised so many times it was unrecognizable from when she started. It would never be finished, never be good enough, but it was all she had.

When she collected the last tooth from the strange kid, she pulled out a dollar bill. Then she hesitated. Before she placed it under the pillow she wrote two small letters next to the pyramid, next to the triangle at the top that looked like an A.

She watched in the morning as the child woke, and, disappointed, plucked only money from beneath her pillow. Then the child looked more closely at the bill, saw the scrawl, and knit her brow.

"RT" she read aloud.

Her pouty lips turned down.

And then, her eyes widened.

"Art," the child said, in a quiet, delighted voice.

She smiled, exposing a blank space where her front tooth had been.

Zan Agzigian

# My Own Tower like Riblet

I could live there,
above the curve of river,
high in the clouds
where nobody sees me
but Minnehaha's
small outcrop of granite

Where I tower in the peaks
of knee deep snow
overlooking the drag strips of
train tracks, behind a big oak door
no one can reach or open

I could live in a castle peak,
amidst a solitary point,
forefatherly flag unfurled,
declaring a country
unto myself,
a rolling cloth
of red

Surrender
Fortitude
Solitude

Pathetic?

Someone has to live there.

Can I?
Why not me?

# Horseless in Spokane

I wish I had a horse here
closest I can get to one is Stacey
horse woman   owner of horses
her hair golden hay

I wish I had one grey and reined
to give these streets more creatured meaning
secretive whole eternal not

So kept, or cracked, or stuffed
on a horse I would be higher
and I'd never have to walk dark

Down these streets alone
nursing every motion with caution
cursing children before they are born

Having a horse would be having you:
that longstretch back of neck for you
are the frame of a street's wide sense

I'd gallop ice hills on highback legs
from train to wood to dream
of brimming riverbend to drink beside

Extincting boughs of brave trees
horse on high pass riding back my back (your back)
a steaming flatbed

Oh, dear, frozen Bigfoot,
I would bow West—horsehooves
in a wintry pause

Curried,
Unforgiven,
to desire, thrust

# Playing the Death Card

Mozart's Requiem with Dutchie the Rabbit,
Spokane Symphony at the Fox

After getting back from Wallace with Wallace the Bear,
I lift this experience up to my rabbit's eye.
Dutchie, born from basket of Tin Man Gallery,
adopted on my own birthday.

Norvel
is unwrapping a Hershey's kiss
for Valentine's and Lincoln's Birthday,
while, with love, the symphony's new
CD plays like mad prophesy.

Dutchie's in my coat, his
ears squooshed. I ask Norvel, "Where is Tiny?"
Left him home, so small, we forgot.

Norvel smooths out Dutchie's ears, says "You will hear better if
they are straight…"
I set our friend out on my lap.
"Exceptional" is Norvel's summary of the
first set of music. We eat kisses, more kisses.

Dutchie's ears are sticking up
from under my arm. He leans in, hand
on my chin, smelling of carrots and horns,
as a requiem rolls in ripples near the
Monroe Street Bridge in 4 movements.
It's a concerto in C with flute and harp,
tears in my eyes, the flute is "C"—
same as mine.

Dutchie, whose attention span is that
of a rabbit's, reminds us that when we get home,
we have a choice of two films:
*Trade* and *Creature from the Black Lagoon*
(both about abduction)

A woman falls. I hear the thud out my
left ear. Dutchie's nose wiggles as I turn.
She is curled in a fetal position on the stairs.
Dutchie asks if we need to help her. He will
hop on out there and do what he can. Her boots have
razor heels. I say, "She is okay. Is she okay?"
Dutchie whispers, "Apparently not."

A man helps her up before Dutchie throws
her a rope in the dark. There are many, like shadows,
lurking. "I'm embarrassed," I hear
her say. Dutchie nods, "I'd be, too,
but then again, I've never fallen before."

Our rabbit goes on to explain how he
can sense when something is wrong.
He could feel the fall in his chest,
like a heart attack: flute and harp,
the heavenly angels descending,
to carry, ascend.

John plucks, and plucks his violin
from his chair on stage as we talk about
tumbling, fumbling, one, two, three:
I count starlights in the ceiling, think
this doesn't always put you at the Center.
Grant us all eternal life, for we praise
Spokane. Hear our prayer.
To us, all flesh will come.

# Crows

Crows fly wide through these red Palouse clouds,
tip the tops of junipers and ride the morning air
in this channel valley, dusted with dreams.

Tulip petals slurp the stony garden stairs,
and temples, bent in prayer.

Shadows, feathers at full spread,
cool the heated, hairy heads of people down below.
Crows
are a creeping wing expansion,
crisp and cool like sheets neat between the toes
of newborn river horizons.

Their monstrous caws lift the foam from waves,
and eddy beds of other sorrows.
They are the only source of soul.
But giants are plucking them from the fiery moon.

Their yellow eyes, soft and mellow,
sweet like citrus in beds of black caviar.
Their feathers are what some men hunt for.

Their beaks are stalks of celery.
Their heads a luscious pie,
better than blackbird.

Jess Walter

# The Mermaid

The summer after middle school, Daryl and Todo and me met this mermaid.

We'd all just moved into Todo's place because he had the coolest mom, Sheila.

Sheila was super fat and had bad eyes. She sat in the house all day a foot from the TV, blankets hung over the windows because the sun made her sick. But she was good to Todo.

Me and Daryl slept on Todo's floor. Sheila said, I only got one rule. Pick up your shit. But that one rule always changed. Don't punch walls. And Leave me out of it. And Don't do nothin' to bring no cops here.

Todd we called Todo because he was a total smart-ass. That's a double negative, he said to his mom. Don't do nothin' means you want us to do it.

Sheila never even looked up from her TV. The *fuck* it does Todd.

But her rules were good. And Sheila never hit us or brought assholes home or stole our money, so we all thought she was cool.

My mom's okay, Todo said, but yours is hot, Mitch.

Sometimes when Todo was being funny it made you feel crappy. My mom was on a bad stretch, her boyfriend turning her out for oxys.

Sorry Mitch, Todo said. I shouldn't of said that.

It's okay, I said.

Daryl's mom we didn't even talk about.

It was the Fourth of July and we decided to watch the fireworks downtown. We were in Todo's backyard when I saw something in a pile of bricks in the alley. I pulled it out. A baggy of leaves and stems. Someone must've hid it there. It was all craggy and brown. We broke that shit up best we could, then we got a Sprite bottle and some foil out of the garbage to make a pipe.

Daryl took a hit from the Sprite pipe and let smoke go in the air. Man, he said, I don't know what this is, but it ain't weed.

We smoked it anyway. Just in case.

And we started downtown.

That's when we saw the mermaid.

She was in one of those plastic pools with the four-foot-high sides that people in our neighborhood put in their front yards. Ghetto pool, ninety bucks at Target, no filter, you just spread it out, filled it and the walls stood up. There were three lawn chairs in the dirt next to it. And just that one girl bobbing like she was treading water, but almost *above the water*. She had black hair and brown eyes. We knew she was a mermaid because she had shells over her titties.

Dude! I said. Are you a mermaid?

She made a squeak like a dolphin. We all looked in the pool and sure enough. Her legs were covered in scales and ended in a fish tail.

You know what I always wondered, said Todo, is how do mermaids shit?

Without a word she hoisted her blue butt over the side of the pool and a turd landed on the dirt lawn. But it wasn't a normal turd. It was an emerald.

I bent over to get the emerald but right before I touched it the thing turned into a normal turd.

Daryl asked, Can you shit other gems or only emeralds?

The mermaid didn't answer. Just hovered in the pool.

Don't mermaids grant wishes? I said.

Mermaids do not grant wishes, she said. Maybe you are thinking of genies. She said all this without her mouth even moving. She just put the words in our minds.

But, she said, mermaids *do* have the power to communicate prophecies.

Todo looked at Daryl and me. You guys want a prophecy?

I didn't really. It was probably gonna be hard to understand. Or a trick. Like she'd say, your dick will turn to gold but then it turns out a gold dick hurts when you pee or doesn't work for sex or something. And what are you gonna do? Break off your gold dick and sell it? Fuck that.

I wouldn't mind some Doritos, Daryl said.

Do you have any Doritos? Todo asked. He was the one with the most power to communicate with the mermaid. Do-ri-tos? He talked slow, like she was from China or something.

Of course, the mermaid said. I have all different varieties. And right between those lawn chairs suddenly was a huge bag of Cool Ranch Doritos that hadn't been there before. We sat in the three lawn chairs, eating Doritos, hanging with the mermaid.

I sure wish we had Mountain Dews, Todo said. But no Mountain Dews appeared. I guess there's rules to everything.

When the chips were gone we stood up. Well, we should get going.

The Mermaid said, You may wash off the leftover cool ranch dust from your fingers in my pool.

No way, Daryl said, and he licked the Cool Ranch dust off his fingers.

Then we started walking away.

We were halfway down the block when the mermaid's prophecy appeared in our minds like some story we'd always known.

You will have great adventures and perform many memorable deeds, the prophecy said. You will automatically know all the cheats for the new Grand Theft Auto. And those Russian dudes in that house on Gardner will no longer fuck with you. Todo, that stuck-up girl on Sinto will agree to tug your junk. And Daryl, you will find your old bike in the weeds behind Bong's Market.

My bike that got stolen a year ago? said Daryl. No way!

Way, said the prophecy.

I was nervous because the prophecy hadn't mentioned me yet.

Oh sweet sweet Mitch, said the prophecy, her voice now soft and kind, like she was putting me to bed. Kind, lost Mitch, do not worry. I have not forgotten you. Your heart is good, but sometimes you get scared. Listen to me. You are stronger than you think are. I want you to remember that. And you are not alone. You can do anything in this world, anything you set your mind to.

It felt like something heavy and warm. We were all quiet, standing there on Boone Street, the words washing over us like a soft rain.

Also Mitch, said the prophecy, your dick is totally going to turn to gold!

I knew it! I said. I fuckin' knew it! I told the guys the trouble with having a gold dick. We laughed our asses off.

Then we went downtown for the fireworks. It was crazy. The guy doing the fireworks show messed up and the whole thing blew up on the ground. Explosions and smoke and shit everywhere. Firetrucks. It was cool. Todo heard later the guy lost a hand. That sucked for him. But still.

That night, back at the house, it turned out Sheila had gone out to the store. She let us scarf a whole box of Pop Tarts and watch Cartoon Network.

On the way to bed I went in to piss. It really did seem like things were going to be okay. And in a certain light, my dick *did* look sort of gold. And it worked just fine.

Shawn Vestal

# The Plowman Wakes

If those are your legs
sticking out of the ocean
then I am already too late
to shake loose my wings
to hail a cab to sell
my blood for magic or money
to slide down shale
and swim to the deep
of the strait and you,
I am sorry to say,
cannot swim.

This is the operation
of the new engine.
The constant burn
of midnight. I am
standing on a hillside
plowing suddenly seems
less important than it once did
I want to say I'm coming
I'm on my way
but I can't speak
or move or plow
the painted earth
any less than this.

# Behind It

Surely that bird has a name, some language
to go with its two-note song, but I don't know it.
And that gray sky, I can think of no word
to describe it, not quite the color
of sheet metal washed in blood, and I have
no idea where that plane is coming from,
the invisible one above the clouds, sliding
through the throat of the sky.

I feel like a speck, a quark, dwarfed,
and that's good. Deep tracks stand
like columns of shadow in unmelting snow.
I set my feet in the tracks.
I am knee-deep in crystal earth,
nameless bird sound, planesong,
that constant sky and the constant
behind it, the pending disappearance
of all things. The sun drops

and there is no moon, only the night's
reflection off the snow, a blue shiver,
and that bird's name is my name,
and its song is called song
and the plane has just landed,
to marching band and ticker tape,
from the town I grew up in,
the year of my birth.

# The Name of the Song

For the longest time, our music
drowns the song of the falls.
Then the roar begins slipping in.

It seems we've gotten bad advice
about where to sail the yacht. Some cry
turn it up, make the music scream,

because maybe we can silence this,
shut it up. We're dressed for a miracle,
after all, in tuxedos and gowns,

the gentlest leathers. We need special glasses
to see the sandwiches, they are so tiny,
so reputedly delicious, spread

with a paste of stewed bones.
We pick up speed, and trees blur
along the shore. Something wants

to crush us against the horizon.
This laughter is sickening, unless
you join in. Falling, the woman

next to me is shrouded in her gown,
and I don't recognize her stockings
or her one remaining shoe.

Below is mist, mist, water waiting
to come into view, and we become
a galaxy of falling things, me,

the woman I know but do not know,
somewhere her shoe, an ashtray,
that tumbling barrel, the captain's dog,

hind leg whipping the frantic air.

# Christmas

The cowshit doesn't smell right anymore.
We all say so. It adds pounds to the air,
clouds the town in things gone wrong.

Cows outnumber voters now. Dairies
sprawl by the freeway, where other places
put hotels. Gangs of cattle, stained and vast.

We remember thirty-six cows.
Every morning, every night.
The clack and suck of the chutes.
The hose and Harley gleam of the tank.
Mom, younger than the youngest of us now,
hauling in a gallon jar every morning,
a thick disk of cream floating on top.
It sat at the center of the kitchen table,
the king of breakfast, two shades of white.

That smell is not right. It comes in
without knocking and handles
the silverware. It sits early for dinner
in a garland of entrails, a crown
of black flies, and it will not shut up.
It says things so plain you are
a fool to need them said.
Yesterday leers like a shill
from an alley. Experience dies
every moment into memory.
Everything, all of it, the smell itself,
fading as it rises.

Marianne Salina

# God's Notes to America

In May 2023, the year God finally retired and moved into a flat here in Brooklyn, everyone's first question was, why'd he do it? Why leave heaven for high rent and hipsters?

I'll never forget the clip they played over and over from the Today show--how God just sat there in a red, overstuffed chair, shrugging his billowy shoulders, letting out a deep, heavy sigh. He closed dark, tired eyes and opened them again. He stared into the camera. It was piercing, watching God like this. He took a sip of what I assume was coffee, though you never really know when it's on TV.

"Well," he said, with a note of sadness in his voice, "a lot of people here are dicks."

And Matt Lauer nodded, as though we we'd all been waiting our whole lives to hear God say it out loud.

"But the ones up there," he said, indicating with his index finger toward the sky, "They bore me to death. And you know, Matt, honestly, when you get tired of heaven, you know it's time to go."

Up until that point, I'd had my doubts about the afterlife—whether it was really something I wanted to invest time and energy into achieving. Because, let's be honest: being a good person is really damn hard work sometimes. But over the next twenty minutes, as God went on to describe and ultimately verify my worst fears about dying and actually *getting into* heaven, well, let's just say I was truly relieved. Answering prayers left and right, eating all the colors of the rainbow, gardening every day, and *sharing* the Cable subscription among what? Hundreds? Thousands? Maybe hundreds of thousands of people at that point? It sounded downright primitive up there.

I felt a tremendous weight had been lifted from my shoulders.

"Do gooders," he said. "The whole lot of them. And really," he said, "there's nothing wrong with that. But I'm tired now. I want to watch the season premiere of Orange is the New Black the day it comes out, and not two months later, you know? I'm just over it up there," he said. "I'm done with heaven for now."

He said he'd worked out a deal where he could still go back and visit from time to time when he needed to. Apparently every dog that's ever died is, as we suspected, up there now, running free.

Now that God was gone, heaven had become essentially another gated community. No new residents, he said. He'd closed shop and moved into a loft in Bed-Stuy. My friend Jake lived just down the street from him for a while there.

At first, for the first six months or so, the twitter feed was full of nothing but God-sightings and clever little aphorisms about finding spirituality in the produce section, where God would invariably be hanging out, choosing from an assortment of grapefruit. There was also a whole new take on selfies. While there were still a good handful of folks posting over-sexed, pouty images of themselves over the Web, the selfie movement had become a little more God-focused, now that he was around. People went out of their way to post pictures of themselves whenever God might be somewhere in the background, maybe tucked into the corner of the photo, next to a parked car, or walking amidst a crowd of people at the farmer's market. Sometimes God would be directly behind the person snapping the picture, but he'd be looking the other way—not necessarily oblivious, but just indifferent. He often wore a faded baseball cap and a sweatshirt, so it wasn't easy to decipher him from any other casual New Yorker, except that God had a sort of radiant elegance in his dishevelment. He sort of glowed a little bit, only not in any kind of halo sort of way. It was more of a yoga glow. And from what I understand, God does do his fair share of downward facing dogs.

He never agreed to photos—not because he was annoyed by them—but because he didn't seem to internalize what this fetishizing of one's own face was all about. He commented on it only once, as far as I know, when a man on the street asked for a picture with him and an onlooker caught the whole conversation on camera.

The video lasts about fifteen seconds on YouTube and it went viral almost immediately. It takes place somewhere on the lower East Side—just a guy asking for a selfie with God, and God shakes his head and says, "No, man. I can't do that for you."

But right as the guy starts to walk away, God reaches out, puts a hand on his shoulder, and says, "Hey dude. I am sorry you have to die someday." The guy looks startled and starts to back up, but God keeps going. "No, hey listen. I know that it's scary, and I know that's why taking all these pictures of your life is comforting to you. I get it," he said.

The guy just stares a couple of big, dumb eyes back at God. His jaw kind of hangs open.

"But you're going to die still," God says. And he speaks really slowly as he says each word, like he's talking to a very young, very fragile, very small child. "Taking so many photos of your own face won't change it and it won't feel good in the long run. I promise you. The death part still comes—no matter how much preserving and archiving you do."

The guy was cool about it, and that was about as preachy as I've ever heard God get. The kind of amazing part of this video was that after it went viral, people kind of took a break from their selfies. It didn't stop completely, but it felt as though the whole country had enjoyed a deep breath and a long, satisfying exhale. A break from themselves. Like the relief that comes after a frenzied, electric storm, when everything suddenly grows quiet and still.

And of course there were all the religious groups trying to cash in on God—begging for a statement that would attach his name to their group, making pleas for an appearance at their church, even demanding that he stand behind one sacred text or another. Was he a Jewish god, was he a Christian god, was he Islamic, or Hindu or non-denominational? He answered none of them. He would politely raise his hand, lower his eyes and say, "Please. Please. Let's stop with all of this now, shall we?"

It was like this with him. Low-profile, baseball cap, shaggy haired God. Just another old guy hanging out. A real down-to-earth bro, if you asked the local baristas. He gabbed with folks on park benches, played a game of cards, a match of chess from time to time. He ordered Ruebens from the local deli and did the Sunday crossword puzzle.

And then, one day, God was gone. The stuff in his flat was all cleared out and it was later confirmed that he had moved onto the next country. God was a New Yorker no more.

All that remained in his apartment was a note—one thin sheet of scrap paper, composed by pen in a wavy scrawl. The letter has since been embalmed for preservation, and is now housed in a fire-proof, bullet-proof safe at the Smithsonian. But I like to imagine it just as it was photographed in the papers: A single note posted to the fridge behind a Homer Simpson magnet. Nothing complicated. Just a to-do list and some expired milk inside that God forgot to toss out. It reads:

God's Notes to America

1. First, my friends, please take more baths. I gave you water mostly so you could heat it up, sip whiskey, and read books inside of it. Really, truly, take advantage of the bathtub. Heaven's got nothing like it.
2. You should see what you all look like when you're planted in the earth. Really. It's hilarz. Appreciate your looks while you have them.
3. Some of you have turned out to be real dicks, and that's a shame. But many of you try hard to be good humans, to be kind to each other. High fives to those guys.
4. I'm telling you: earthly pleasures are where it's at. Read your books, watch your movies, eat your food, love each other well and have lots of sex. Have sex during thunderstorms, have sex in the middle of the desert. Love each other until your skin grows thin and your bodies expire. This is it. It's as good as it gets.
5. Clean up when you're done.
6. I'm on my way to Palau. Heaven can wait.

Peace out, God

Melissa Huggins

# The Lost Girl

*"As if in answer to his request, the air was rent by the most tremendous crash he had ever heard… The roar of it echoed through the mountains, and the echoes seemed to cry savagely, 'Where are they, where are they, where are they?' Thus sharply did the terrified three learn the difference between an island of make-believe and the same island come true."*

J.M. Barrie, *Peter Pan*

The night Audrey was kidnapped by pirates, the island had been quiet for hours, with only the rustling of trees and the distant roar of the river to keep her company. Every so often, she could hear gnomes scuffle in the underbrush or the scream of a mouse as it was snatched up by an owl, but those sounds were familiar. As the eldest, she was always the last to go to sleep, keeping watch from the hammock she'd set up above the entrance to their network of caves. When the other girls thought to ask why she stayed up so late, she winked and told them she wanted to protect them from her loud snoring. She'd have told them anything to get them to sleep, but the girls believed her, especially in the comforting light of day when any number of games and adventures were already taking shape in their minds.

That night, thick clouds obscured most of the stars, making it harder for her to pass the time. One of her favorite games was to pick out which stars were part of the famous stories. Was it that little bright one who called out to Peter Pan when he nearly flew into the path of a mortar launched from the *Jolly Roger*? Did that winking group guide Tink as she rushed to inform Peter of Hook's plot to poison him? Perhaps the flickering one at the very edge of her vision helped light the way for new children when they arrived for their first terrifying night in Neverland.

Audrey knew the old stories, of course—all the lost girls and boys did. Since Wendy Darling had been the original storyteller, Peter expected her daughter and her daughter's daughter and her daughter's daughter's daughter to do the same, so when they were old enough, he brought them from Outside to tell stories and mother the lost boys. He, of course, never remembered any of the stories himself, and Audrey suspected he didn't really notice a difference between the generations of Wendy-girls he convinced to fly to Neverland. He was as likely to forget you were standing next to him as he was to remember your name, but nothing brought him more delight than being told a story of his own adventures—especially the ones where he thought he'd been especially brave or clever.

But those weren't the only stories. Audrey knew others, ones she would never let the other girls overhear. There was the time two mermaids drowned a boy because they were tired of him throwing pebbles at their tails, and the time one of the girls stepped on a hill of killer ants. They swarmed her so fast that they'd already filled her throat and suffocated her before her body hit the ground. The mermaids had even whispered to Audrey that from time to time, Hook used to capture a mermaid and keep her in a tank in the captain's quarters on the ship. Eventually he'd tire of her and order his men to cast her back into the sea. The mermaids who'd returned didn't like to talk about their imprisonment, though if pressed they'd admit that while he'd never so much as dipped a pinky finger into the tank, somehow after being with Hook they felt a great sadness bloom in them that persisted even after returning home. Many of the girls reported waking up to find him staring at them. Nothing improper, of course—he was ever the gentleman around ladies, such a stickler about good form—but they'd catch him staring intently at their faces, as if he might find the face of someone he once loved.

Sometimes Audrey dreamed of being in love, but she'd never had the queer sort of feelings for anyone that Tink and Wendy and other girls had for Peter. She'd never given or received a kiss—thimbles or otherwise—but she supposed that love meant feeling safe and cozy and wonderful all the time, like how the lost children who could remember their mothers said they used to feel as sheets were tucked around them and kisses planted on their foreheads at bedtime.

She couldn't remember her own mother, nor did she long to be one, but lately she couldn't shake the feeling that as much as she loved Neverland and the lost girls, something wasn't right. At odd moments she would feel quite clearly that she didn't belong there, but since she didn't want to grow up and have a lot of babies and live a plain life on the Outside, she wasn't sure what those feelings meant. In the meantime, she continued inventing new games for the lost girls, making dolls for the little ones, and practicing her bow skills. Peter, she knew, imposed such a lot of rules on his boys to make sure they never stopped believing, but she had never done so, leaving room for the girls to decide for themselves when to eat and when to go on adventures and when to pretend and when it might be time to leave their small tribe. She never said a word when they started to show little nubs of breasts through their shirts or played games where they pretended to have a real baby of their own, in a real house with real servants and a husband and a dog. She just waited patiently for them to come to her, and when the time came, she told them the way and asked a fairy to accompany them back to the Outside.

As Audrey gently swung in her hammock and brushed away a firefly, she felt her eyes closing of their own accord, her head nodding to the side. Each time it happened, she had no sense of whether minutes or hours had passed, only how heavy her head felt, and she closed her eyes again almost immediately. Once, she thought she saw a fairy out of the corner of her eye, but she told herself she must have imagined it, or perhaps mistook a bat swooping by. Soon she was overcome, and surrendered to a deep, uneasy sleep.

When she woke, she found herself on a dingy cot in a tiny cell, enclosed by iron bars on three sides and a wooden wall behind her. The cell had a narrow swinging door just wide enough for one person, which was fastened with a padlock. Across the room sat Smee, singing a little song to himself as he sewed the hem of a large panel of red fabric.

*The sharpest coat he's ever had*
*A garment fit for kings*
*The softest fur, the brightest red*
*what luck this jacket brings*

Smee's narrowed eyes rose from his work to meet hers. "Awake at last," he said. "Cap'n wants to speak with you."

It wasn't long before a tall, broad-shouldered man strode in the door. Long black hair cascaded around his shoulders in curls that would be the envy of even the most precious little girl, but somehow, combined with his uniform—a sharply tailored jacket over a loose, white shirt tucked into fitted pants, along with sleek black boots—the hair actually made him look more imposing, like a wild animal whose movements you couldn't predict. Audrey shivered, though with fear or anticipation, she wasn't sure.

"Welcome to the *Jolly Roger*, my dear," he said without a trace of irony.

She could feel the ship undulating softly under her feet, but she couldn't tell whether it was anchored or in the open sea.

"I owe you my sincerest of apologies," he continued with a deep bow. "It seems you've arrived on our ship quite by mistake."

Smee grunted, shifting the fabric on his lap. The captain glared at him.

"These imbeciles misunderstood my orders," he said, "which were to spy on the inhabitants of the caves, not to apprehend anyone."

"As your prisoner, I have the right to know what's to become of me," she said.

"What do you expect?" the man asked. He walked closer to her cell, stopping a few feet away, arms behind his back. He was close enough that she could see the crease lines on his forehead, notice the bright blue of his eyes, and tell that his curls were wet, as if he'd just bathed.

"Am I to be forced to join your crew?" she asked.

"Do you think you're strong enough?" he asked. She had the disconcerting sense that he knew her answer to every question before he posed it, and that he asked only to observe her as she answered.

"I'm strong enough, and old enough, too," she said. "But I should much rather be returned to the lost girls."

"All children have to grow up eventually," he said.

"Except Pan," she said.

His face betrayed nothing.

"Except Pan," he repeated, not sounding like he believed it. He gazed at her for a long beat, as if taking a moment to evaluate the course he'd selected, and then, "My dear, we'll discuss your future later, after we get you settled into more appropriate accommodations. You have my word no harm will come to you on this ship. But I still haven't properly introduced myself. My deepest apologies. Captain James Hook, at your service."

When Audrey disappeared from the caves, the other girls assumed she'd gone on an adventure. Perhaps, they guessed, she was searching for the long-rumored penguin colony or climbing Bear Mountain. But after a handful of nights—they weren't sure how many—when the littlest ones woke up crying at the wolves' howls, they enlisted the help of the fairies, who called a meeting of the island's inhabitants. Nearly everyone was represented: a group of drunk pirates on shore leave, two of the native tribes, the mer-people, and the fairies; the wolf pack, the lion pride, the sleepy owls; even the notoriously deceitful gnomes and the tiny old mountain woman who could appear and disappear at will. But it quickly became apparent that no one knew or would admit anything, and the gathering devolved into open combat. Fearful amounts of blood were shed, without anyone quite remembering why, and still no one noticed that the *Jolly Roger* was no longer anchored off Neverland's coast or thought to wonder where it had gone or with whom on board.

Years later, as a grown woman, she could still remember the feeling in her chest as his eyes searched for her reaction to his name and he reached through the bars to politely shake her hand. It was as if her lungs had been gripped in a vise for all her life and she'd had no idea what breathing really felt like until the pressure had loosened ever so slightly. She was surprised, of course—everyone thought Hook had been dead for years, gobbled up by the croc—but also she felt glad, for no reason she could have identified at the time, as she watched him extend the hook through the bars ever so carefully, turn it sideways, and use his left hand to enclose hers between the warmth of his good hand and the cool metal of the other. Looking into his eyes was like a freefall, exhilarating and terrifying in equal measure, and the more she stared, the more she felt that if she gazed long enough, she might understand all there was to know about him without exchanging a single word. But in that moment, before they set sail together and said tender things, before she abandoned the lost girls, before James gave up pirating; long before they lied to one another and even longer before they tired of each other for good, all she could feel, thrumming through her whole body, was *yes*.

Samuel Ligon

# The Little Goat

There were once a girl and a boy who lay on a hill of gravel kissing until their lips were raw. Kissing was the best thing that had ever happened to the boy and the girl, and so they rode their bicycles to the gravel pit every Sunday in pursuit of that sweet, singular pastime.

One Sunday, the boy pulled his t-shirt over his head. He kissed the girl and the girl kissed him back and then the girl pulled her t-shirt over her head. The girl didn't have much need for a bra, but her grandmother had taken her bra shopping in the spring and now the girl wore a bra every day, whether she needed it or not. Without her shirt on, the girl wanted to crush herself against the boy. The boy could not believe the girl's radiant smoothness. Her bra was a miracle. It was like a bikini top, but it was not a bikini top. It was the girl's bra.

The girl ran her hands over the boy's back. The boy ran his hands over the girl's back, over her harness and its hook, which he finally opened. The girl sat up and lowered the straps from her shoulders. The boy put his hand flat against one of the girl's breasts and then the other. Her breasts were warm and soft and the boy thought touching them was the best thing that had ever happened to him. The girl watched the boy's face, his hands on her breasts. Later, when she pressed herself against him and he pressed himself against her, there was nothing between them to interrupt their skin and they kissed each other until their lips were raw.

In July the girl went to the seaside with her grandmother. The boy couldn't see the girl then and the girl couldn't see the boy and they both thought they would die from not seeing each other. Awake and asleep, they dreamed about the gravel pit, about kissing and taking off their shirts and crushing themselves against each other. July was awful.

But in August, the boy and the girl were reunited. They lay on their bed of gravel kissing and taking off their shirts until they could hardly breathe. The girl felt a feeling in her chest and the boy felt a feeling in his stomach. They kissed each other and ran their hands over each other. The girl liked the way the boy's hands felt on her body, creating a kind of leverage for their crushing. The feeling was like butter about to run, butter still holding its shape but about to melt completely. The girl loved the smell of the boy and the boy loved the smell of the girl. He loved her touch and she loved his touch. They breathed each other and touched each other and kissed each other until their lips were raw.

Neither the girl nor the boy saw or heard the little goat descend the gravel hill they lay upon kissing. Neither smelled the goat as it approached. Presently, the little goat stood alongside them, watching them kiss and touch. It cleared its throat, but the girl and the boy were lost in each other. The little goat lowered its face to their faces and bleated.

The girl and the boy jerked upright. They jerked upright and away from each other.

The boy struck the little goat's snout, and the little goat bleated again.

"What do you want?" the girl said, covering her breasts with her hands. "Why are you here?"

"You're not doing it right," the little goat said.

"Doing what right?"

"What you're doing," the little goat said.

"Get out of here," the boy said.

The little goat had slitted devil eyes.

"We don't want you watching us," the girl said.

"Are you ashamed?" the little goat said.

"It's private," the girl said, "what we're doing."

"This is a public place," the little goat said.

"Nobody knows this place except us," the boy said.

"It's a free country," the little goat said.

"No it isn't," the boy said.

"Wait," the girl said. "I think I know this goat from a fairy tale. I think we're going to become rich and famous." She turned to the goat. "Bleat my little goat, bleat," she said. "Give me something good to eat."

Nothing happened.

"I'm not that goat," the little goat said.

"Which goat are you?" the boy said.

"A different goat," the little goat said.

"I'm going to kill you," the boy said, picking up a handful of gravel.

"Don't kill him," the girl said.

"He's ruining everything," the boy said.

"He's harmless," the girl said. "And kind."

"He's not kind," the boy said.

"I'm really not that kind," the little goat said.

"Still," the girl said, and turning to the boy: "You know how I feel about animals."

The boy did know how the girl felt about animals.

"All right," the boy said. "Can we go back to kissing then?"

"Not with the goat here," the girl said.

"You're not doing it right anyway," the goat said.

"That's none of your business," the boy said, and the goat said, "What do you think my business is?"

"How would I know?" the boy said.

"Are you a spirit goat?" the girl said. "Are you supposed to represent something?"

"No," the little goat said.

"Don't you know when you're not wanted?" the boy said.

"I have every right to be here," the little goat said.

"No you don't," the boy said.

"You're both using too much tongue," the little goat said, "if you want to know the truth. Back off a little. Get a little more air into your kissing. A little more breath."

"I'll make a stew of you," the boy said.

"I think he might be right," the girl said. "About the air."

"He's not right," the boy said. "About anything."

"Let's try what he said," the girl said.

"With him here?"

"It's okay," the girl said

She lowered her hands from her breasts and pulled the boy into an embrace.

"This just feels so—"

The girl kissed the boy.

"Breathe her breath," the little goat said.

"Shut up," the boy said.

"Also," the goat said, "you're going to have to take off your pants."

Still kissing the girl, the boy grabbed the goat by a horn and twisted its head.

"You're hurting me," the little goat said.

"Ignore him," the girl said. "But I think he might be right about the pants."

The boy let go of the goat's horn.

He kissed the girl and breathed her breath, and the girl breathed the boy's breath too, kissing him.

"All animals do this," the little goat said. "There's nothing special about it."

"Kill him," the girl said, still kissing the boy and breathing his breath.

The boy kept kissing the girl as he twisted the little goat's head by a horn.

"Ouch," the little goat said. "Listen to me. There are other things to do."

"We know that," the girl said. "We don't need your help."

"You don't know anything," the little goat said. "You need plenty of help."

"We hate your guts," the boy said, twisting the little goat's head.

The girl kissed the boy and pushed herself against him.

The boy kissed the girl and pushed himself against her.

The little goat bleated, a mournful sound, like a child crying.

The boy and the girl could hardly breathe.

"Let him go," the girl said.

"Let's go somewhere else," the boy said.

The little goat bleated.

The boy twisted the little goat's head by a horn, causing him to crumple in the gravel.

"We should take off our pants now," the girl said.

"Yes," the little goat said. "You can kiss with your pants off."

The boy twisted the little goat's head until the little goat bleated again.

"You're hurting me!" the little goat cried.

The girl unbuttoned the buttons on her shorts and slid them off.

"Let him go," the girl said. She touched the waistband of the boy's shorts. "Take these off," the girl said.

The boy let the little goat go. The girl's panties were a miracle. They were like a bikini bottom, but they were not a bikini bottom. They were the girl's panties.

"This is one of my favorite parts," the little goat said.

"Shut up," the boy said.

"You can watch," the girl said, "but you can't talk anymore."

"All right," the little goat said.

The girl watched the boy slide out of his shorts.

Everything was about to happen.

The girl slid her panties down, watching the boy watch her, hungry and murderous.

The boy helped the girl climb on top of him. He could smell the girl's sweet smell and he could smell the little goat and he could smell something he'd never smelled before that made him feel desperate. The girl rubbed herself against the boy.

"Now we're talking," the little goat said.

"Pay no attention to him," the girl said. She was heavy and light, full of air and breathless.

The boy had his hands on her hips. Everything was going black around them, with her sparkling at the center, her face a face he'd never seen before as she lowered her mouth to his, darker and more beautiful than any human face he'd ever encountered. He breathed her breath and she rubbed herself against him and then it was another thing entirely as she enveloped him, his hips moving with her, knowing now what to do and how to move, the two of them fluid and rolling, inside and outside, sweat and their mouths and their bodies hot and liquid and fully contained, salt, blood, meat and butter, and yes, the girl thought, and yes, the boy thought, and they could hear each other breathing and growling and falling out of time completely.

Then they lay together, breathing their own breath, stuck and sticky against each other.

"So now you know," the little goat said.

"Don't think I won't kill you," the boy said.

"Do we become famous now?" the girl said.

"No," the little goat said.

"Why do you want to be famous?" the boy said.

"I don't know," the girl said. "I just do."

The boy felt a feeling in his stomach.

The girl pulled on her underpants.

"Leave those off," the boy said.

"All right," the girl said.

"Let's do it again," the boy said, and the girl said, "Let's always be doing it."

Neither of them could imagine anything better than what they were about to do again. Neither of them saw the little goat climb the hill of gravel and disappear.

Ann M. Colford

# The Man in Black

Miss Amanda—none of the neighbors know her last name—sits on her porch in a rocking chair, sipping jasmine tea. The tea in her china cup has grown tepid, but she doesn't mind. The rocker creaks upon the wood of the porch floor, eking out the first two notes of Miss Amanda's favorite old hymn: "Lift high … Lift high … Lift high."

Her house, a tidy white clapboard cottage, is an anomaly in the neighborhood, sitting a few feet from the street, its tiny lawn bounded by a white picket fence. Ivy wraps the porch pillars, and petunias spill from hanging baskets. On either side, rundown houses and apartments shoulder together, front doors spilling their work-worn residents onto the weed-strewn urban sidewalk.

A hawk calls out as it soars in a lazy spiral against the overcast sky. Her eyes lift to follow the bird's flight. A hawk? Here in the city? Must be lost, she thinks. She knows they hunt the bluffs along the river, but what is it doing up here? Her grandmother held superstitions about birds of prey—they were portents of evil, she'd said, drifting up from the unsavory riverfront and rail yards. The raptor swoops low, searching for food in her scrap of a front yard, then sails out of sight.

Amanda hears a voice growing closer with short, sharp, agitated cries. Her eyes travel to the end of the block and spy Benny, one of the neighborhood's characters, roiling in her direction, all helicoptering arms and legs. Everyone on the block knows Benny and knows he's prone to alarm. He's never been quite right, ever since—well, for a long time. But he's a good soul, if you can overlook his excitability. Always seeing demons, Benny. And always trying to convince you that you see them, too.

"He's coming!" Benny yells. "Miss Amanda! He's coming! Stay on the porch!"

Amanda sees the fervent light of both panic and anticipation in Benny's eyes. If she didn't know him so well, she'd swear that he'd really seen something terrifying this time. But she knows better.

"Now, Benny," she says, "you don't have to worry about me. When was the last time you saw me out there on the street?"

"But he's coming this way!" Benny continues, barely pausing at her gate. "He's looking for you!"

"Who's coming, Benny?" If she could get him talking, maybe she could figure out what had set him off this time.

"The Man in Black," Benny says in a stage whisper. "He's coming, Miss Amanda. He's coming for you." With that, he was off to warn the rest of the block.

Silence echoes in the wake of his departure. The resident robins and sparrows have gone mute. Even the hum of city traffic has stilled. In the distance, Amanda hears the hawk cry.

A figure appears, approaching down the middle of the street—tall, clad all in black. The man's boots drum a slow rhythm on the blacktop. At Amanda's gate he turns, without a pause. He closes the gate behind him then stops and lifts the brim of his hat with a black-gloved hand.

"Ma'am," he says. His voice is deep. In that one syllable, Amanda hears railcars and steamboats, saloons and prison cells. He bends forward to pick up something in the weeds: a feather, striped brown with white. He takes two steps forward and hands it to her over the porch railing.

"A gift," he says. "A sign, from the river hawk who sent me."

"Sent you?" she says, holding the feather between her thumb and forefinger like a quill.

"Yes, Miss Amanda," he says. "Sent me to you."

Well, she thinks, twirling the feather. Benny's reports of calamity have finally proven accurate.

"Do you know me?" she asks.

"Our spirits have soared together before," he says. "If you will... walk with me, I will explain."

"Walk?" she says. "You mean... out there?"

He nods and reaches a hand toward her. "Please," he says. "We have much to share."

She meets his eyes. Yes, she sees boxcars and prison bars, but country churches and swaying choirs as well. She set the feather down on the porch rail and rises from the chair. Steadying herself, she straightens her skirt and adjusts the scarf at her throat. The man's hand guides her down the steps, like she's a grand lady descending a coach. She slips her arm through the crook of his elbow, and they pass through her gate. The sidewalk welcomes her feet. A soft breeze wafts the feather into the air, up, up, into the currents and away.

Kerry Halls

# The Big Black Cat with the Dark Brown Mane

There was a kind little girl who lived on the outskirts of Spokane with her mother. Though she lived far from other children her age, and her mother was always very cross, the girl was never lonely, for there was a big black cat with a dark brown mane that came to visit her every day. In the mornings the girl hid pieces of egg and bacon from her own breakfast in the pockets of her jumper to share with him. When she returned in the evening from collecting firewood and huckleberries and mushrooms in the forest, the cat greeted her with a purr and a series of tumbling tricks in the dirt pathway behind her cabin. And at night, as she fell asleep, he would sit outside her window and sing lullabies from cat kingdom.

But the girl's mother hated the cat. She didn't want him eating the food she cooked in the morning. She thought his tumbling routines kicked up too much dust. She didn't care for the sound of his singing voice. So one day, after the girl left to do her chores in the woods, the girl's mother replaced the pieces of egg and bacon she'd left behind with poisoned bits and waited for the big black cat to arrive. After he ate his breakfast, the girl's mother leapt from her hiding place and exclaimed, "You foolish animal! I have poisoned those bits of egg and bacon. I'll not suffer your presence again after this day."

"But what about the little girl?" the cat choked. "Won't she be lonely when I'm gone?"

"Better lonely than cavorting with a lay-about like you. Now get on," she said, shooing the cat with her foot. "The last thing I want is a dead cat on my property."

When the little girl came home, the cat was nowhere to be seen. She called and clicked her tongue. She checked under the porch and behind the shed. She snapped her fingers and made rustling sounds in the leaves, but he would not come. Distraught, she turned to her mother. "Have you seen the big black cat with the dark brown mane?"

"I have not bothered to look," she lied. "Perhaps he's grown bored with your company."

But it was not like him to disappear, and the girl would not relent until her mother, angered by her questioning, confessed. "I poisoned that filthy beast this morning," she snapped, "he's long dead by now, and good riddance."

Crushed, the little girl fled to the woods to find the animal, to apologize and give him a proper burial. She searched and called and cried as she wandered, until she was lost deep in the pines.

Finally she came upon a little gray cat, grooming himself on a moss-covered boulder. "Excuse me," she said politely, "can you help me? I'm looking for the big black cat with the dark brown mane."

The little gray cat stopped his grooming and looked at her incredulously.

"Please, little gray cat. My mother poisoned him this morning. I want to apologize and give him a proper burial. He was my friend."

The little gray cat sighed, turned, and began walking toward the river, cocking his head in a way that invited her to follow. They walked until the full moon floated high in the sky, and came upon a dense thicket of very tall cattail plants. Inside the thicket were many cats, peering from their modest homes, but the little gray cat led the little girl past them all to the grandest home in the center of the village. When they arrived, the front door opened to reveal the big black cat with the dark brown mane.

"My mother told me she poisoned you!" she cried, hugging him fiercely. "I'm so sorry."

The cat gave the little girl some warm milk and a bowl of sugared huckleberries to ease her nerves. He purred deep in his chest as he explained his journey home. How the other cats of the kingdom wailed as they watched their king, poisoned and dying in the village center. How he'd been fortunate to have one of his nine lives left to spare him the fate the little girl's mother had attempted to deal. How he'd devised a plan to repay the little girl's mother for her treachery.

The next morning the little girl returned to her cabin with a small satchel of gold. A gift from the king of the cats, she told her mother. An offering of friendship and piece, she told her mother. A smaller bag than they had originally offered, she told her mother, as she could not lift the large bag they wished to give.

Her mother's greed rose as she imagined what the large bag must contain, and she demanded to be led to the cat village so she could claim the gift that was rightfully hers.

When they arrived, the big black cat with the dark brown mane greeted the little girl's mother with a bow, but she had no interest in niceties. "Just bring me the large bag," she barked, "and we'll be on our way." The cats did as she asked and she left, not caring that the little girl had stayed behind.

The large bag was heavier than the mother had anticipated, and the walk home longer than she remembered. She stopped half-way to rest her weary limbs and steal a look at the treasures she'd been given. But as soon as she loosened the drawstring at the top of the bag a deafening gust burst forth from the opening, and she recognized at once the true nature of her prize--the collected lamentations of the cats in the village as they grieved their dying king. Every cry, every yowl, every wail twisted around her like the tail of a golden snake, its feline head rising before her. She tried to apologize for her wrongdoing, but it was too late. The golden snake with the feline head opened its jaws wide, letting out one final, piercing cry before devouring the mother whole.

The kind little girl remained in the village of the cats, where the big black cat with the dark brown mane and his subjects performed tumbling tricks for her and sang her to sleep for the rest of her days.

Bruce Holbert

# Marriage
## A Fairy Tale

We shall begin the old way. Once upon a time, Claire, my wife of eighteen months, studied the want ads for houses. I had never purchased anything worth more than a used pick-up, but Claire wanted a house, so I put down payment on a place on a dirt street that held three similar properties along with a development for the indigent.

Claire stood before the out-of-fashion split level crying, but not for reasons I'd hoped. Tongues of pink paint unlicked the wood siding. The stoop's crossbeam sagged under a failing foundation. Inside, nicotine pasted the walls except where the summer heat had sweated it free in long brown beads. In the hard-packed dirt even dandelions found no purchase. Roaming dogs rooted trashcans and scattered the contents along the street.

The next day, Claire shopped for paint, brushes, and rollers and spread faded bedding for drop cloths. For a month, she primed and enameled rooms. Finally, she edged and trimmed the last wall and unmasked the switches and baseboards, then hesitantly tapped studs and drove nails for photographs and brackets and placed the knickknacks from her hope chest along the cupboard shelves until all they possessed animated each room.

She persisted, leveling the porch with house jacks one week, trading out the frayed shudders the next, then wire brushing and painting the siding. I assisted when she asked, mostly instances that required lifting or turning rusted screws or reaching eaves from the ladder tops that she couldn't. She borrowed a rototiller and broke the yard into furrows, then raked them flat and spread seed and set the oven timer to alternate sprinklers. Too late in the year to start annuals or vegetables, she buried iris and tulip bulbs along the house beds for spring.

Evenings in the vacant lot behind the house, children and their mothers swore like Longshoremen. I played music or switched on the fan. Claire filled her ears with cotton balls. However, one child's howl could not be quashed: a five or six year-old girl with ratty blonde hair and a voice to peel bark from trees and a face blank as the white sky. In one hand, she lugged a Barbie, rumpled as herself, which she employed to clobber the threatening dogs that emerged from the willow's shadows.

Early autumn, Claire informed me she carried a child. The next day, she ordered cedar slats and hired a hardware crew to fortress the house with a tall board fence. She admired how they drove posts, chalk-lined them level, then hung the stringers and hammered slats into rows.

I cannot recall what moved me to join the reclamation project, and, if I could, it would probably not be the truth, but, to my wife's surprise, the hardware delivered a second time that afternoon: planks and two-by-fours on the lee side of the house. The next night, I dug a foundation and poured footings to anchor a deck I had sketched on a grocery sack.

Nights, Claire printed lists of baby names then alphabetized them in gender rows, with a smaller group down the center that could go either way. One might conclude I felt left out, but I nickname any person I know past hello, and expected a child in my house would have several monikers beyond his or her first. Order for me was the tavern menu and if it changed there was always a cheeseburger. For Claire, however, it was insurance she could purchase with effort and foresight.

So, I too, I toiled happily the days that followed. Typically, I am a hasty man with no bent toward precision or caution. The deck planks, though, I measured twice to cut, then squared each end with a triangle. Perhaps the prospect of turning girders and trusses and struts into something a wife and child could stand upon with my own hands slowed my frenetic mind and quelled my character flaws.

Winter approached and I had managed the deck bearers and floor joists and a ten-by-twelve lattice to shade the west portion. Beyond the fence, the children surrendered the vacant lot to the cold and the gaunt dogs with ribs in bladed rows.

One night, late, Claire listened while they attacked an unfortunate cat. I plunked at them with a deer rifle but missed, and they dragged the cat to a thicket and feasted.

One evening I glanced up to find the ratty blonde girl searching my lunch bucket for sandwich dregs. In the house was a bowl of apples and I fetched one, which she ate. The next day I warmed her a thermos of hot soup and she volunteered to press one end of measuring tape while I marked a cut. After, she collected the scraps in a metal burning barrel. The next evening I fed her dinner's leftovers and paid her with pocket change and a couple of ones. Her name was Rose, though I called her Silly Putty.

The fetus stretched in Claire's womb and she wrapped around it the way a nautilus protects its chambers. I touched the shifting baby, but only through her skin, and my diluted experienced could not rival hers. Claire completed the child herself, as she had the walls and shelves.

Our first altercation during her pregnancy was over the fence gate. I propped it for the child, which Claire didn't abide.

"You know why I ordered that hasp," she said.

"Yes," I said. "And you know why I undo it."

I carried on with the deck flooring. Rose had become passable hammering short nails and familiar enough with the toolbox to deliver what I needed. I bought her a second-hand coat and wool mittens at the Goodwill. One Saturday afternoon, we attended the library puppet show; we visited a fountain to throw pennies and next the greenhouse, places most would call plain, though Rose's narrow face turned fierce with attention. I invited Claire to accompany us, but she remained busy with baby clothes and a birth announcement, sans name and date.

Mid-March, a Chinook wind thawed the ice and snow over a long week. Claire, just short of her time, pressed for a dinner in town. On a shiny late afternoon, I set a sandwich on the wood piling with fifty cents for Rose, but Claire latched the gate behind us. It was a slight cruelty, not directed upon the urchin, but me for dividing my attentions.

The dinner was the most enjoyable evening we had spent in months. We sat on the same side of the booth and held hands and I felt almost the man I hoped to be.

Home, the car lights illuminated the driveway, then the house and fence. A shape lay heaped against the metal door as if blown by wind. It appeared a blanket or heavy tarp, but I recognized the child's bloody jacket shredded by the dogs. I lifted the girl and carried her to the car. Claire hurried herself from the passenger side.

Several hours later, I returned. I heard Claire call out from the bedroom but did not reply. In the hall closet, I collected the axe and the rifle and that night I killed eleven dogs and beat the leader into a fenced corner with the axe handle. I cleaved its skull with the axe blade.

I showered and, the next morning visited the hospital. A bandage cap protected Rose's shaved scalp and a hundred forty raised red stitches divided her face. I called her name, but hearing my voice drove her to howl until her cuts seeped and I was asked not to return.

After, I saw her only when I passed the bus stop where she waited with the other children. Scars wandered over her face and she stared past me with stone eyes, and if I lived a hundred years I knew I could not outlast the silence she meant for me, a silence that seeped into my house like bad weather and into my marriage, though neither Claire nor I spoke of the loss, even a month later when our own child, delivered crossways, stymied and died within her.

Laura Read

# The Goose Girl

On her handkerchief, she carries
three drops of blood
and they tell her,
*If your mother only knew,*
*her heart would break in two.*
But she doesn't—only the girl knows
and the geese she drives out deep
into the country, like the secret
I tried to tell my mother in the garage
about the older boy
in the closet
who laid me down
under the openings of dresses.
But I could not say it—
it would be like all the geese
lifting at once in their perfect V,
the suddenness like something
breaking in the kitchen and she says
*What was that?* and I say, *Nothing*
and sweep up the glass.
The king knows something is wrong,
so he asks the goose girl
to tell her true story
but she can't, she promised,
so he says, *Tell it to the stove,*
and I think of our green oven with the light

where you can watch the bread rise.
I could put sticks in there and light them.
But these are not my wet boots
sticking in the marsh or my geese
lighting on the pond.
When they honk, I can hear the quiet,
how deep it is, and empty
like the old boxes in the hall closet
from JC Penney and the Crescent,
which is closed now, its windows empty
of snow-flecked carolers and deer turning
their mechanical heads.
We used to stop there and stare in,
and the sidewalk glittered,
and the lamps came on.

# The Little Mermaid, the Long Version

At naptime, you always want me
to tell it, the whole story of Ariel and Eric,
but we've already been to the park,
cut the crusts off sandwiches,
watched the men on the roof next door
attach the vinyl siding.
It's the yellow of the butter melting
in the glass dish in our cupboard.
You try to mix the right color on your brush
while I lie on the floor next to the basket
of clothes. The day is so slow
we can watch the leaves unhook themselves.
Your brother grows up out of me
like a knob on a gourd.
When we finally lie down together
on your moon-and-stars sheets,
I can only tell the short version
before falling asleep: Ariel loves Eric.
She dreams of legs, sees her body splitting
at night in her clamshell bed.
So she goes to the sea witch who says,

*If you give me your voice.*
This is the part you like best and you sing it.
Then I say *Now her tail will split*
*and she will have three days to make Eric love her.*
This is not enough, but she is beautiful,
her hair flows in the air like it's still in the water.
I don't tell you the ending I know
from the books I listened to
on the tape recorder that rang a bell
when it was time to turn the page.
I sat in the corner while the fan whirred
and the trees leaned their shadows
against the house. Eric marries
somebody else and the little mermaid turns
into sea foam. Her body is the bright line
of green that keeps washing up in ribbons.
This is the long version. I can hear her
out there in the water, the sea-hum in her throat,
her fingernails scraping the sand
as she tries to hold on with every wave.

# Briar Rose

Sometimes you do something you shouldn't.
Like when I told the mother I was sitting
next to at the sixth grade graduation
that I was sad my son was leaving

elementary school, and she patted my leg,
and I said *No, you don't understand,*
and she held her cupcake mid-air,
and I said *It's over.*

She glanced at her small daughter
who still had years of tracing her hand
to make a turkey at Thanksgiving
and her teacher wearing her Grinch slippers

to school on Dr. Seuss's birthday
and those weeks every fall
when the homework was Moon Viewing,
which my husband said we never did anyway,

it was always too late when we remembered.
Still I wanted to, I wish we had drawn
the moon every night so we could see
how it was always a little different,

I told the woman, and by that point,
she was staring at me, but I just kept talking.
Sometimes I think he should just go
already, so college won't be always out there

like a storm. Haven't you always hated it
in movies when one character calls out
after another but doesn't follow?
Sometimes we do what the story requires.

Like in the fairy tale—they know
the girl is supposed to prick her finger
on the spinning wheel on her fifteenth birthday,
but they leave her to do it anyway.

I remember the first time my son really saw
the moon, I said, when I could see the woman
thought I was done. He was a baby,
and I was holding him in one arm

while I opened the car door with the other
when suddenly he opened his mouth and made
a sound, the kind of sound that just slips out
when you see something beautiful.

Nicole Sheets

# H is for H-berry

The maiden's mother died, and her father married a Christian Pilates instructor named Kelly. While the father was away at a conference for hospitality industry professionals, Kelly banished the maiden from the house. Don't come back, Kelly said.

"Can I take my rollerblades?" asked the maiden.

"Yes," said Kelly.

The maiden kept herself alive on the water from nearby streams and the expensive vitamin supplements Kelly sold to support her Christian Pilates studio, Holy Moves. She rollerbladed for several days until she came upon a letterpress studio.

A printmaker opened the door. He could use another set of hands in the shop. He didn't make a lot of money and had no friends other than a marmot who slept in a plushy heated bed, the kind of bed usually reserved for a pampered cat or small dog. The marmot opened one eye to look at the maiden, and then rolled over to face the wall.

"You can be my apprentice," the printmaker said. "Also I just finished this stir-fry. Would you like some?"

The maiden nodded and grabbed a plate from the cabinet. She seemed to know where everything was without having to look for it. Even the printmaker, who'd emptied the dishwasher countless times, had to open a couple of drawers to find a colander or a corkscrew.

The printmaker was at work on a book about the flora and fauna of his homeland. As he printed each page, he left space for the big initial letter, like something from an illuminated manuscript, which he'd paint by hand under a full moon. Basically, this book was taking forever.

The printmaker loved his homeland. Wonderful things grew there, but you had to be patient. It was like waiting for a full moon, the kind of moon you paint by.

The maiden had a good eye for design. She'd suggest small changes to the layout of the type or to those large, ornate capital letters. The letter needs a shadow, she'd say. Of the tree in the giant P for Ponderosa: not so many branches, she'd say. About the R for River: the water should look wetter. Helpful things like that.

The maiden liked to play with words. She would make up songs of words she'd overheard her father and Kelly talk about, exotic words like Jacuzzi and Bacardi. Sometimes she'd include words like Palouse and Basalt that she'd learned from the printmaker's book.

One morning the printmaker came home with a tub of little pudgy purple buttons. The maiden had never seen these before. He ate a few and then gave some to her and the marmot. "What are they?" she asked. He wrote the word huckleberry on a piece of paper. She giggled because he was being so secretive about it, like a child passing a note.

"You can't say this word out loud," he said.

"Is it a bad word, like douchebag?" she asked. Kelly had been very firm that no one under her roof would say douchebag or even the abbreviated d-bag.

"These are magic berries," the printmaker said. "They grow wild. No one can tame them. They're always listening. Don't say their names out loud, or you'll unleash their dark magic upon your immortal soul."

The maiden cracked up.

"Listen, I'm serious," he said. "Don't say it out loud."

"OK, OK," she said. She ate a handful of berries and resumed her usual incantation. Jacuzzi Bacardi…

That afternoon at break time, the maiden challenged the marmot to some Wii bowling, as usual, and the printmaker chopped some vegetables for the crockpot.

Usually the maiden beat the marmot without much effort. He would sulk and think about pooping in her rollerblades, and she would go back to work. But today, he was on a roll. After his third strike in a row, the maiden shouted, "Why, you little h-berry!"

She knew it was shadow swearing, the kind of thing Kelly would punish by making her spend the afternoon bottling homemade kombucha for the church fellowship dinner.

The printmaker stopped his chopping and cleared his throat. "You're pushing it, young lady. Do not call down that berry magic upon your immortal soul."

A full moon shone that evening. The printmaker was busy, painting his luminous H surrounded by huckleberry bushes. A small bowl of berries sat on his worktable for inspiration. The air was humid, threatening rain.

The maiden snuck into the kitchen and ate the last of the berries. She stuck out her purple tongue. "Huck huck huck," she said. She wanted that word. Why couldn't she say the word?

"What's he painting tonight?" asked the marmot as he fished out a Sprite from the bottom of the fridge. "And hey, can you open this for me?"

The maiden grabbed for the can, popped the top, and over the hiss of the spume answered, "Huckleberries." In an instant, thunder boomed right over their roof, and the lights went out.

The next morning, the printmaker couldn't find the maiden anywhere. Her rollerblades were by the door as usual. The marmot banged his empty food bowl on the floor. The printmaker stirred a pot of porridge on his propane stove.

A breeze fluttered the manuscript pages on the worktable and scattered them all over the floor. The marmot strained to reach the wooden spoon poking out of the porridge pot. He stirred in little jagged karate motions. Oh, how he hated burnt porridge.

The printmaker ran to the workroom to rescue his pages. He gasped when he saw the painting he'd finished the night before. The berries had exacted revenge. The maiden had taken their name in vain, those wild berries that the guidebook described as "perfectly poised between tart and sweet, excellent in pancakes and also a mojito." The maiden was caught in this flat, gilded world of bushes and berries, under one lonely cloud, at the top of a mountain, at the foot of the big leggy H.

Brooke Matson

# The Monster

Ivy springs up everywhere—
stowaways in the roots of lilies
given by a friend who believed
she was giving me

only beautiful things.

Now deep-green dragon tails
are twined with every flower,
cunning as cancer
and quick to spread.

We are surrounded, darlings.

There is no escape from the monster's tentacles.
The sun will slowly grow
farther away until
your slender voices drown

in the body of another.

# Tomato Vine

It was a question of love:
the pale green orb appeared
this morning, clinging

to a pungent umbilical branch.
What had been a crumpled blossom
had turned inside out overnight
and began swallowing

water
in what I imagine
to be a last

gasp for existence.

Faithful monster—

dedicated little
heart of seeds—
fill your tight skin with

every blessed drop.
Stay connected

to the vine. Stay
at all costs
connected.

# On the Zambezi River

The truth is, I was barely ready to see them.
I had been drinking on a boat.
I was young and tired from teaching in overcrowded huts.
The weekend was supposed to be a break,
but the three of us had done nothing but argue
over trivial things.

I'd isolated myself on the upper deck
where Texan tourists were singing drunken songs.
If the sky was pitch and stabbed with stars, I didn't notice.

The steward who poured my drink
had said, *You look like an African lady,*
which I thought was strange because if anyone could blend
into a white wall, it was me. Thinking of this, I noticed
the light on my glass was not
from a lantern on shore, but the moon.

It was gigantic.

A marble dome sitting on the earth.

I watched it for a long time.
The tourists kept singing.
And then they came—

distant but clear, their movements shattered with light
on the river, walking right across the moon,
trunks swaying in the rhythm of their slow march.

Even as I clicked the lens of my camera, I knew this picture
would never turn out (which
it didn't). So I burned it
in my mind: the silhouettes
of those great and gentle beings
trailing one another across the light
and I wanted to cry

because I was in love with this country
and hated its poverty and violence—

even as it brimmed with laughter
and beautiful women with calloused hands
and jungles and moons and majestic creatures.
Perhaps that is what the steward read in my face.

They were gone. The moon

began its slow leap from the water.
I wasn't angry anymore.

When I found the others I told them
what I'd seen:  elephants crossing the moon.
"Wow," they said, and turned back

to complaining about the Texans,
whose rendition of *Bye Bye Miss American Pie*
had reached intolerable volume.

Polly Buckingham

# The Ghost Fair at Panamint City

Marina knew Milo was waiting on the crooked porch, that he'd been there since two hours before dawn, because that was the time of the night he couldn't sleep. He was out there with Magic whispering to the burro, trying not to wake her, though the whispering was so loud, she could hear an occasional word, "Ferris wheel" and "freak show." Surely there'd never been a Ferris wheel in Panamint City. How, in 1890, could they have possibly driven it up through the canyon waterfalls, even with a twenty mule team?

The pot of water she'd put on the coals in the woodstove was finally boiling. These last coffee grounds, acquired from a four day trek to the one gas station in Trona a year ago—or two years ago, or six months ago, time had gotten difficult to count—were her last. She had to admit, Milo's incessant chatter about the ghost fair had intrigued her, or terrified her. Would interacting with that many ghosts amount to the same terror interacting with real people did? It wasn't that way with Milo, but then, he was only eight. Children were easier. Impervious. Concerned with themselves. Sweet no matter how weird you were. Weird themselves, really weird. And ghost children, well. They hid behind rocks or played strange games with sticks and sang 100 year old songs to themselves. None of them spoke to her, just Milo. She wasn't convinced they even saw her. If the ghost carnival people didn't see her, the carnival might be wonderful. The coffee grounds were wrapped in a thin piece of cloth tied with a string. She dropped the little ball into her one metal cup, a prize found in one of the handful of abandoned cabins.

"Okay, Milo." She swung open the door, but instead of Magic a man with a Playdough face sat beside Milo on the stoop.

"He's from the carnival!" Milo said jumping up. "He's the painter."

"Ma'am." His face was shy and red; his eyes looked right into hers. She immediately looked away, though the moment of contact stretched like a dry lake bed so flat and endless you can't possibly measure the distance.

"His name's Joe. He comes first. The painter always comes first. He's gotta paint the paintings of everyone arriving, and the Ferris wheel getting set up."

"There's a Ferris wheel? Really, Milo?" she said, surprised to hear her voice, casual, unwavering, as it always was with Milo, incredulous, the way you challenge a child who's likely passing off a story as the truth or the truth as a story.

"Maybe there is a Ferris wheel. You don't know. There could be a Ferris wheel. One boy told me about a Ferris wheel once."

"Here? Up the canyon? Six miles, 5,000 feet up? Pulled by mules?" It was like the man wasn't there, even though he was. It was like he wasn't watching her, even though he was. It was like she wasn't wondering if maybe she'd fall in love with him, even though she was falling in love with him. She hated love. But even so, here she was, talking to Milo just like she did every morning, the boy who doesn't age, even though she does, talking with him just like no one else was there. And not wanting to crawl inside her skin. And not being scared he, this stranger, this painter, might touch her, even a handshake, might notice her, which he did, she knew. She could feel that.

"Well, even if there isn't a Ferris wheel, there are other things he paints. Like the freaks. He paints all the freaks and puts the paintings outside the tent so you want to go into the tent. Like the Dog Lady and the Fat Man and the Camel Boy. He painted a skeleton man once, and he said he really was a skeleton, no skin. Isn't that right, Joe? Didn't you tell me that?"

The man nodded.

"He could paint you, Marina. He said he could paint us both. We're the people who go to the fair. You gotta paint those people cause there'd be no fair without the people who go. Who'd pay the money? But you won't have to pay money at this one. I mean, what would anyone do with money? And anyway, they probably won't see you."

Marina looked down into Joe's face, looked right at him, stunned by him looking back up at her with his sleepy eyes.

"She don't look at no one, Joe. I told you that. I told you she'd like you. Didn't I Joe?"

"That coffee?" Joe asked.

"Maybe it still has the taste of coffee," she said. The taste of coffee like a memory. A memory of mornings in the other world, the world outside of Panamint City, outside of Death Valley. The world populated by people where the houses had real floors, and woodstoves had doors, or there were no woodstoves but real heating instead. Houses with electricity. Houses she'd felt trapped in. Except for those quiet sunrises in whatever backyard, on whatever porch, walking down whatever empty road. Memory of the one good thing. Everything here was empty, and there were no structures that made her feel trapped—just broken cabins and a hundred or more stone foundations, walls, empty doorways, the memory of structures. And there were no people. Just the ghost children.

"Marina," Milo said. "Please can't he paint us? Joe, you'll paint us right? Isn't that what you said? You told me that. I know you did."

"Course I will," Joe said. His eyes were brown and clear; in them she saw the story of a fair painter who falls in love with a hermit one hundred years older than him.

In the other world, she'd grimaced when anyone asked her to smile for pictures. "You always look like you're about to cry," her sister had complained. "Why can't you just be normal and fake smile like everyone else?"

"Okay," she said. Because she wanted to know, what does he see, this ghost painter from 1890? When the silver town was in its fullest bloom, a couple thousand people, enough to support a fair. What would she see?

She sees the rest of the story in his eyes as she holds her memory coffee standing in the doorframe of a dilapidated cabin, the rugged wildflowers in bloom all around them, a burro eating grass, the mountains purplish, the air dry and dusty and sage smelling: ghost painter falls in love with crone, leaves her, of course, because that's what painters do when the fair is over. He leaves behind the painting of a woman in a filthy v-neck tee shirt, her skin a mosaic of brown and black splotches, hair bleached white from the sun, face swollen, eyes slits surrounded by crow's feet, an astounding blue the painter will notice and will focus on so that looking into her face is like looking out at an ocean where a vast salt flat should be.

Marina looks away from the painter. Magic the burro is grazing. She wonders, not for the first time, if ghost burros taste what they eat, and which of the other burros are alive and which dead. She wonders what happens to the painting painted by a ghost painter on a canvas made of fog, when the ghost painter leaves.

Maya Jewell Zeller

# Ordinary White Room

At dusk her aunt the witch
swings into the ordinary white

room on her broom. She's hungry.
She's wanting something like root

vegetables, something papery, a grub
or snake skin on a casserole of nails. The girl

sends her to the cellar for a jar of rhubarb,
a potato or two, the closest things she has

to witch food. Her aunt's straw broom leans
in the corner, by the window, where it points

to the moon. The girl wants wild. She wants
to feel the whipping alders and then the wisps

of mist fogging her eyes. She wants to hear
the croaks of frogs blended in the blue luminary

basement of dark. Her aunt is taking a few minutes.
She could be doing anything down there, digging

strings of glowing nightshade-root lights from holiday
bins, changing spiders into men to massage her feet.

The girl takes the broom between her legs.
She can smell the night floating toward her,

like someone who comes back from the creek
with a bucket of water and salmonberries to share.

He has a cold chest, warm breath. He's more than
a constellation. She opens her jaw wide enough

to put her mouth over a star.

# When a Mind Becomes Conscious

Today the picketers stood outside our gates
with signs saying a human life begins
when its mother is born. Do they think

we don't love our mothers? Or that we
have forgotten the children we could have
someday if we were allowed to leave?

When we walk past the fences on our way
to the garden they shake their fists in our faces
and say we're crazy because our doctors

put faith in science over God. I have never
met God, and I don't trust science, either,
its slippery tadpole in the palm. What

appears to have a tail can lose its tail
and grow legs in a matter of weeks.
We watched the frogs crawl from the barrel

of rain water last night and some of us
cried. We remember walking in the lands
beyond these walls, remember our lives

when we had a different kind of grasp
on consciousness. In particular, I recall
watching the current take baby turtles

and spin them, their shells keeping them
safe from debris. This was before I knew
smell. When water still kept things I felt

smooth beneath my fingers. My doctor
says these memories are a fabrication
of my ill brain. She says I dreamed

this life, that it was never a conscious
state, that probably someone molested
me or I spent summers in a vacation

home on the shore. She tries to help
me identify familiar childhood scents,
orders me a variety of foods that might

trigger reality, makes marks on a chart.
When they bring me sushi, I unwrap
the rice and meat and eat the seaweed,

strip after strip, the beautiful dark damp
of it, its salt so perfect my mouth can hardly
believe it is real. I tell her we called it sea

hair, that it grew freely of its own accord,
we ate only what we needed to eat,
and that, as a child, it was my first food.

# When They Scanned My Brain For Love

It was the animal that came up
dominant. The animal who tears
across the lawn at dusk and leaps

into the pond. The animal who climbs
trees on the property perimeter,
who sleeps in the leaves,

dreaming of anemones and starfish.
Who walks barefoot toward the sea.
I can hear it wrestling with the sand,

that old game, swallowing and choking on
and spitting out glass. It smoothes,
but doesn't feel tender toward stones.

The sea came up dominant in me—
not a field, or sky. No wonder.
These qualities lie just beneath

the scalp–self esteem, veneration,
benevolence. When they scanned
my brain for love they found only

my longing to come and go and
repeat. My currents pulled
by a world beyond the one

they know. I would pullout my hair
for that world.

# Herman Hesse Says The River Is Everywhere at Once

Because the river
never really leaves our house,
even after the floodwaters

recede and the bath tub
stops filling with silt;
and the yard, its grass flat

and littered with rusted
whirls of barbed wire
and logs and baling twine

and ruined books, begins
to regain its pastoral shape;
because the river never really

leaves even as it leaves
these things, I breathe water
in my sleep. I breathe water

as mist, as rain,
as the undercurrent
where clouds of minerals

swirl in and out of the same
circles, where the captain
keeps his hopes, a chromophore

catches fire. It looks a lot
like the cross-section of a cell.
I can cut from one end

of the room to the other
with one tail flip.
The river is everywhere

it has ever been, which might
mean I am, too, completely
capable of starting over,

or going back, my body
and this house both absolutely
submerged. We're underwater,

we're so lucky to be full
of matter, I'm not human,
I'm surrounded in seaweed,

I'm finished trying on dresses,
eating these strange grains,
I'm done with these sun-drenched

days, I'm everywhere
I have ever been, I'm getting
out, I'm getting in again,

I'm getting gills, I'm getting naked,
I'm getting my feet wet
*at the source and at the mouth.*

# January 9, 1493: Columbus Mistakes Manatees for Mermaids

What is there to love
about Christopher Columbus?
By now we know he was a liar

through and through: pretending
to have fallen into a new world
through the rabbit-hole of the ocean,

to have found this place where thousands
already spent their days living,
where mountains knew the feeling

of feet on their backs. Or so I have
read. I know so little. But I can tell you
Columbus told the truth

about one thing. Those were no
manatees he saw off the coast
of the Dominican Republic. The story

goes that my great great great
grandmother and her sisters
swam to see the ships with pretty

names and came back ashamed.
So I've been marked with the curse
of curiosity. It's genetic. Once

I traveled to see the aftermath
of a tsunami. I couldn't keep up
with the waves themselves. Water

is the only thing that can travel faster
than a mermaid. The beach where
those large swaths of sea crashed

down was still awash in foam.
There were dead babies, floating,
and I couldn't save them. No one

even seemed to notice my fish
tail, my glowing hair. They were
already in another world.

Kelly Milner Halls

# Responsbility

"Where are they?" Mother asked Sister.

Yet another household item was missing. Blaming Sister was easy. Brother was younger and far more likely to misplace things, but the thought never crossed Mother's mind.

Sister pushed broken glasses up the bridge of her nose and answered, "I didn't use the toenail clippers, Mother. Did you check in the pewter bowl?"

"I've looked everywhere," Mother snapped. "If they're not back by the time I get home from work, young lady, plan on cleaning every toilet in the house. You must take responsibility for your careless actions."

Sister willed the tears in her eyes to retract as she stared at the broken laces in her sneakers. "I'll find them," she whispered, without a clue of how she'd accomplish this magic.

"You'll be cleaning potties," Brother sang to the tune of "Ring-Around-the-Rosie."

Sister glared at him.

"Look at him that way again," Mother said, "and you'll do all the laundry, too."

Sister resigned herself to babysitting Brother, as she always did in the summer. But three hours into the day, the clippers were still missing. "Outside," Sister told Brother. "That's the only place I haven't looked."

With brother settled happily on the swing beneath the Ponderosa Pine, Sister searched underneath every rock and leaf, behind every tree stump. She'd all but given up when the sheen of silver metal caught her eye. Mother's toenail clippers lay on a bed of pine needles at the edge of the woods, huge piles of fresh nail clippings beside them.

"Who took these?" Sister said.

A large furry hand with beautifully trimmed nails appeared above the hedge.

"Bigfoot," Sister said as the eight-foot creature loomed before her. "I knew it."

Bigfoot toed shyly at the pine needles.

"You shouldn't take things without asking," Sister scolded. "It's irresponsible. And you almost got me in trouble."

"I'm sorry," Bigfoot answered. "I didn't mean any harm."

"You should have asked first," Brother whined.

Bigfoot smiled at the boy. "Brother?" he asked.

"Monster," Sister replied.  "Want to borrow him?"

"Yes," Bigfoot said. "Always wanted a family."

Sister smiled as Brother's lip began to quiver.

When Mother came home, she found dinner on the table and the nail clippers in the bowl where they belonged.

"You found the clippers," she said to Sister. "Good job."

Sister beamed.

"Where is Brother?" Mother asked, examining the broken swing on the kitchen counter.

"Is he missing now?" Sister said. "Guess I know what I'm looking for tomorrow. But don't worry, I've already cleaned the toilets AND done the laundry, just in case."

For Sister, taking responsibility was finally worth it.

Nance Van Winckel

# Auditions for the Undead—TODAY ONLY!

A lurching gait, a transparent face,
a screech that opens hell's door—
all must be believable at the end
of an era that's worn vestments
of explosives under a gaze serenely
certain of god's love. Here's
the form should you want to
show us the strut of your stuff.

Give us the best of your worst
death. Go armless. Stand legless.
Make us gleeful with fear. Be good
at devour. Better at re-die. Send forth
the protoplasmic dots of yourself
upon a sky great with clouds. Receive
all blessings but let none stick. Lead us
into the silence of a deeply drawn breath,
which for the rest of eternity
shall never find release.

# Reckoner

You open your mouth—wide, wider—
and voilà, a foggy forest
slips out. Open again and spit
a castle. And so on . . . for a moat,
a stable, and the ever
sallying-forth dead aunties.

Sure, you can spew a distant fire-chucking
volcano. Or blow a spit-bubble
with a baby in it. What language,
what words will said baby let fly
when you're nowhere? When you're
roaming *her* dreams with *her* dear deceased
(& why were *hers* all ball-gowned up?),

when you're a dirt speck in an earth clod
in a world that's eventuated . . . back to
warlessness, back and back to only rats
in the underground, back back back
to fowl becoming fish.

Spit ye more then whilst ye may.
Disregard the 3-eyed, 50-fists-flailing
monster who's right now shouting
through the thin ashy air for you
to shut it shut it shut it.

It seems to me when you were last home we sat around the old kitchen table while Buddy demonstrated a new game he'd invented. Nobody believed anything would ever come of it. Ha! Now he's about to sell it to a big company, although he's "not at liberty to say which." The game involves plastic blocks and tiny little "knights" who, on a toss of the dice, inch toward the center of the minotaur's labyrinth. We all told Buddy what he'd designed looked more like a fancy English garden maze than a labyrinth. Plus, it was clear to the naked eye how to get those knights into the center—and then safely back out. The "real" labyrinth, I insisted, has a blind dark passageway around every corner. Dead ends suddenly appear. And through the centuries many a child has cried in that place. Hedges and cliffs, caves and watery caverns. All at once a child will realize she is NOT dreaming but is fully awake and alive and living the last moments of life. And the moments are suddenly overflowing— as she knew they would be— with everything, EVERYTHING!— they told her not to fear: the mouth, the teeth, the hard tongue that slaps and stings and sucks you down.

I understand Buddy's company is the one that makes the little squares, which by the way, were exactly the sort of garbage we Homer Club gals used to find out there on the pot-holed stretch we "adopted" of Badger Road.

Beth Cooley

# Of a Different Color

Susan had thought it was all a myth, the so-called separation anxiety mothers feel, or pretended to feel, when their kids go off to kindergarten. But now that Donny was almost five, she knew it was real.

"Maybe we should home-school," she said to Joe.

"Susan. We've talked about this."

"But he's only four."

"Five next month. He's a big boy now."

Donny galloped around in the back yard throwing a tennis ball for Alice, the collie. He had been a surprise, a gift, a miracle, after seventeen years of marriage and four miscarriages. Rosa, his biological mother, had come to live with them from a ranch in Idaho, battered and abused. Some cowboy—yeah, they knew who he was—had tried to break her, and when she arrived she was moody, unpredictable and addicted to sedatives. They cleaned her up and worked patiently with her until she could function again. Even so, Susan didn't realize Rosa was pregnant until she delivered Donny right there in the paddock. He was breech, and Susan had to pull him out with her bare hands, legs first.

"Jesus Christ," Joe whispered staring at the baby in Susan's bloody arms. "What's wrong with it?"

"Nothing at all." Susan put the infant down in the hay. She remembered the Parthenon Friezes and Chiron from a Classics course she took in college. She remembered the Beethoven segment from *Fantasia*. "We'll name him Adonis," she said. "Because he's absolutely perfect."

Baby Donny opened his eyes, let out a cry and raised his arms to Rosa. Then he struggled to stand on his four wobbly legs as Rosa bathed him gently with her long pink tongue.

❧

Donny spent his first summer in the pasture nuzzling Rosa's teats and romping with the foals. His baby fuzz gave way to a sleek gray coat and glossy tail. By first frost he was weaned and trotted up to the house several times a day for meals. Susan bought him warm hoodies from the GAP and ordered Greek cookbooks on Amazon. She learned to make spanakopita, baklava. By the time he was twelve months he was speaking in complete sentences. By three he was asking difficult questions.

"We should call his biological father," Joe said one afternoon.

"The cowboy? Are you crazy? That man is a beast."

"He has a right to know," Joe said and took his phone out onto the porch. Susan wanted to eaves-drop, but she stayed inside washing the moussaka ramekins until Joe returned not five minutes later. "There's no talking to that man."

"What'd he say?"

"'So, I made another one.' That's what he said. Then he told me I could sell him to the circus."

"That bastard! Donny's not some freak!"

"Of course not!" Joe said. "Still, he *is* sixteen hands high."

"What are you saying?" Susan demanded, but Joe just looked out the window at Donny ambling dreamily around the backyard listening to his iPod.

After dinner Susan walked down the dirt road to Donny's favorite pasture. Light drained behind the Chiwaukum Mountains as she climbed over the metal gate. Donny stood alone, the screen of his iPod casting a pale glow on his face. Horses rustled and nickered in the shadows around him. Overhead, constellations pricked the sky, Andromeda, Draco, Pegasus.

"Hey," she said. "You out here star-gazing?"

"Yeah, I guess." He pulled off his earbuds and stuck them in his shirt pocket. Lately, his voice startled her, it had gotten so deep. Nothing like your average four year old. And the beard beginning on his strong chiseled chin? Okay. So, he was different, but he was still her little boy.

"Finding any to wish on?"

Donny sighed, "Maybe."

Susan wondered what he was wishing, but she was afraid to ask. "It's about time to hit the hay."

"In a minute. I need to hear this one song."

"Who are you listening to?"

"Katy Perry," he lowered his eyes, bashful. He'd had a crush on Katy Perry for quite a while. Was that normal? Who could she ask?

"Five more minutes. Then it's lights out." Susan's voice caught on the last word. What was wrong with her, going to pieces over his silly pop-star crush?

"Night, Ma." Donny leaned down to kiss her hair. "I'll be in real soon." She looked up into his deep brown eyes, patted his withers and walked back to the house alone.

It was late when he came in. Susan heard him clomping around in the old garage. They had cleaned it out and converted the space for him when he got too big for the little room down the hallway from their bedroom. She lay there in the queen-size bed listening to Joe snore, listening to Donny singing softly as he got ready for bed, wondering where he'd been. Maybe she ought to scold him for being out so late, but he'd always been such a good boy, so gentle, so sweet. She finally fell asleep about the time the rooster crowed.

"The cowboy may be a bastard, but he's right," Joe said the next morning. He was sitting at the kitchen table with his laptop and a cup of coffee. Donny was outside, throwing the Frisbee to Alice and cantering after her. "It says here that there are more of them."

"Them who?" Susan asked sharply, but she knew. For years she'd heard rumors, but she'd folded them up and put them in the bottom drawer of her brain with all the things she didn't want to think about. Her miscarriages. Donny's lack of friends. Rosa's chronic addiction to equine anti-depressants.

"*Centaurs*." Joe pronounced it like a foreign word. "Wikipedia says there's a herd of a hundred or so up in the Chiwaukums." Wikipedia? Great.

"A herd?" Susan tried to steady her voice. "Did you say 'a herd'?"

"A colony. Or community. Other. . .s like him."

"And?" Susan glared. "He's only four!"

"Not in horse years."

"Sixteen, then. Seventeen. But he's not even shaving yet! He has a crush on Katy Perry, for Godsake!"

"That's what I'm talking about. He needs friends, maybe a girl-friend. Someone who can teach him about his own. . ."

"His own what, species?"

"Culture. I was going to say culture."

"But who's going to cook for him? Who's going to iron his shirts?"

Joe bunched up his mouth the way he did when he had something important to say. Or something unpleasant.

"What?" Susan said.

"I got a call from Ray Whitehead. Seems Donny's been hanging around his corral."

"Since when is that a problem?"

"Since his little girl Leda started training that filly of hers."

"Leda's not a little girl anymore. And the filly's two years old."

"Yeah. That's exactly what Ray said." Joe reached for her hand. "Suzie, it's time to let him go."

⌒

On Donny's fifth birthday Susan bridled Rosa and climbed onto her bare back. Since the day Donny was born she couldn't bear to put a saddle on the chestnut mare. Mounted, she was tall enough to meet Donny eye-to-eye. Joe walked them to the gate holding Rosa's reins.

"You got your phone charger, son?"

"In my backpack with Mom's baklava."

"Let us hear from you as soon as you're settled."

"Will do, Pop." Donny shook Joe's hand then leaned down for a quick hug. "You'll come visit, right?"

Joe nodded, unable to speak. He blew Susan a kiss and gave Rosa a little smack on the haunches. It drove Susan crazy when Joe did that, but Rosa didn't seem to mind. She and Donny trotted out the gate. All afternoon they jogged steadily toward the Chiwaukum peaks through woods and open plains. When they reached the foothills at sunset, Susan could see figures moving along the bluff, blurred and dream-like in the amber light.

"Well, I guess this is where you drop me off," Donny said. Susan wished he were a little less excited about leaving home, but there would be plenty of time for feeling homesick later. Not that she wanted that for him.

Or maybe she did. Just a little.

"Bye Rosa." Donny stroked her forelock, and Rosa whinnied. "Bye Ma," he gave Susan a kiss on the cheek, then spun around and galloped off, full tilt toward the shadowed mountains.

Kathryn Smith

# Starvation Couture

I have torn this life out at the seams
and reshaped it. Our clothes
hang like sacks
on a line from our shoulders.
Bone pegs. Wind-
billowed. No cords to cinch our shrinking
waists. This is wilderness fashion.
Sister, don't give me
that pouty expression: so last
year. So gaunt and wanting. Shoes
are so completely out. I mean,
so out we cut away the soles and
boiled and ate the leather.

# Where No Crumb
# Can Save You

In the stories, children wander the woods alone,
falling to the trap of sin. There are ways
to survive. You cannot let the witch
lure you with her house of sweets.
You cannot fear the wolf. I am the girl who

plies the forest with darkness as her ally.
I dig the traps with my own hands, bare. I
am ready to wrestle the lion, just as the Book
prepared me. To emerge unscathed after I've
shared its bed.

# The Transcriber's Daughter

I fall asleep each night to the sound
of pen scratching parchment as she copies
her alphabets, one hundred variations before sleep.
Her day begins with the recitation
of the Transcriber's Oath, emphasis on Rule No. 5:
*The blotted out fall away as though unnamed,*
and No. 12: *In special circumstances, a new name*
*may be given.* I was raised to keep account
of every insect that crossed my sill, to leave
no petal untallied. Once I pressed daffodils
between pages of the Book of the Dead. Now dried sap
blurs the entries, my mother's meticulous hand.
I was thinking of gravestones with their quick-fading
blossoms, the transient beauty we offer the dead.
Maybe this flower, pressed before fading,
would comfort some restlessness, the ghosts I feel
tucking against me in sleep. They whisper my name
in a lullaby until I dream of reincarnation, accidental
in the book's yellowed margins, reborn as one
who sees herself in every rising shoot.

Keely Honeywell

# The Rose Hotel

When they cleaned out their dad's house, her sisters had fought over everything worth anything. Once she'd found the boxes of photos, maps, brochures, and miscellanea from the summer road trips she and her dad had gone on, she was done. She packed the boxes in her car and left.

She and her dad had gone on their last road trip just before middle school. Once puberty had hit her, there were sports to play and boys to chase during the summers, and the trips stopped. That was also when the divorce happened. Her older sisters weren't interested in roughing it in a glamourless roadside motel or a campsite with vault toilets, and without another parent around she and her dad couldn't take off like they used to.

Now she was on one of their old routes, with a new tent in her trunk and their old map on the passenger seat. It was the fourth day into her journey, and she had been following a storm for the past several hours. Just as she reached the little town of Beaumont, she caught up to the dark clouds and they started tipping their buckets. Without a promising glimpse of blue sky ahead of her, she pulled into the only hotel in town. It had the same woodsy look to it as it had years ago, and its sign, a slab of wood with a faded red rose engraved on it, read "Rose Hotel." In one of her dad's boxes, stowed in her trunk next to the tent, was a photo of her next to the hotel sign, wearing a terribly bright pink pair of shorts, her white-blonde hair in a side ponytail.

She was soaked in the distance between her car and the hotel front office, which had an old-fashioned bell attached to the door to announce her arrival. Wiping her hair off her face, she greeted the man behind the counter. She was happy to see the place was still owned by the same family as when she'd last visited. The man at the computer, though, looked supremely bored and was unaffected by her arrival. He rested his chin in his palm as he stared at the screen.

"Do you have a room for tonight?" The parking lot was empty, but it was her usual starter question.

"A queen standard is $75 a night."

"Alright."

They exchanged cards: his paper for her to fill out, hers plastic for him to swipe.

"I stayed here once with my dad," she said as he tapped at the keyboard. "It must have been your dad running the place before. You two are practically identical!"

No response. She remembered his father had been as ruggedly handsome as the Rose Hotel's outdoorsman decor, but she had been twelve and he must have been thirty-something. Now, though, there were two thirty-somethings separated by a counter.

"That rose looks really nice." She pointed behind him, to the single garnet red rose propped up under a narrow glass dome. It must have been cut recently, it looked so perfect. Or maybe– "Is it real?"

"Very."

He still hadn't met her eyes.

"What was your name?"

He looked at her so blankly she thought he might have forgotten his own name. How long had the last customer been in and how long had it been since one of them cared to talk to him?

"It's John."

"Nice to meet you. I'm Belle."

Now that he had finally looked her in the eyes, she felt a little dopey but she would tell anyone that she saw a little of his soul. Just that small piece tugged at her like a vortex in a backyard pool. It sucked away her train of thought.

"Well, um, thank you," she finally said.

The bell rang again as she left the office. She grabbed her backpack from her car and glanced back inside on the way to her room. Through the rain-blurred glass door, she could just make him out behind the counter. He was still staring ahead of him but the boredom had been lifted from his face.

That night she settled into bed with a book in hand but had barely turned one page when she dozed off. Her thumb was still in the book when she heard howling. Not off in the distance howling, wolf right outside her door howling. It woke her with a start but once she realized what the sound was she wasn't afraid. It wasn't like a wolf could open her door. And even though she told herself she was anthropomorphizing, the howl had sounded sorrowful, regretful. She did peek outside, but never saw the crying wolf. If she had, she might have tried to console it.

The next damp, weakly sunlit morning she found a covered tray outside her door. Taking it inside, she was amazed to uncover a full breakfast: eggs, potatoes, toast, all perfectly warm, and fruit, perfectly chilled. That most certainly never happened the last time she'd stayed at the Rose Hotel with her dad.

After savoring what turned out to be one of the best breakfasts she'd had in a long time, she left her room to go down and express her gratitude. As soon as she came into the office, the bell on the door frame jingling, John looked up at her. His eyes were bright and there was a cautious smile twisting up his mouth, as though it were out of practice. Yesterday's dark rain might have tainted her judgement, but the rose under glass had improved to become a blazing red.

"Good morning, Belle."

She instantly decided to stay another day. Or more. Probably more.

Ellen Welcker

# "Are you half-dead after a complicated journey?"*

when I was girl a girl a little monster frightening to be small or a girl a small girl *are* you a girl? or small in the world? I would think to myself when I was a girl are you real and small and a girl in the world? on your way through the day some day any day so plain and near or far from home so safe not safe for a girl little girl in the frightening world a girl I would think a monstrous girl this girl that is if she was a girl a small world girl who strayed one day from her path in the world strayed in the world like a girly little girl little monster girly girl so small and unfurled

---

* Bhanu Kapil, from *Incubation: A Space for Monsters*

# Call this one Princess Extraneous, call him Little Prince

god did god have plans his plans were the children having fun in a golden place safe were they safe with god and bright was it brighter with a batch each batch of classmates new classmates and what were what were god's plans would we would we be together again in the mean the meantime she has made me made me a blank person blanker person so eat I'll eat away I'll eat Subway on her birthday I'll do acts do an act of kindness for kindness minds the mean reminds the time in the meantime your face in the meantime statistics in the meantime status quo the collective unconscious the decision to un-know, recall: without a name, you disappear

Inspired by the *Princess Abandoned* essays, by Kim Hyesoon (trans. Don Mee Choi), & language taken from childrens' obituaries who died in the Newtown school shooting

# "Do you want to see my dead-face?"

if you can  "blood"              "blood coat"
if you can "guns"                "guns magic"

    "guns magic"                  "guns magic"
    "blood"                        "blood coat"

    if you can wish                  you can play dead
if you can still                 you can die

if you can spell "I love humans"     you can love humans

fling                            powerfling        laterwish
    you weren't a human

if you can "guns"                "guns magic"
if you can "monster"             you "monster"

I "monster," fling:

    wind-bullets mud-bullets sunlight bullets
    eyes closed, tongue out, head back

---

My four year-old is just beginning to play with the idea of magic powers—we sometimes freestyle on what kind of magic shield or overruling power would be sufficient if you are on the receiving end of some dark magic flung...

# "The schools have been shot up for more than a year"*

The world is meant to have no top. The air is meant to provide an inner stirring. The footsteps, just now, are veering from the hall. Easier to plan for the post-apocalypse than to wrench the collective pulp and tremor toward a now unnervingly new. The darkness in children is often over- looked by those who squint at the sun. I brought the gun from home. I bought the gun. I brought the gun. I brought the gun.

---

* From an 1863 account on Wikipedia's "List of School Shootings in the United States"

# "the gun was exploratory, another way of getting to know him"*

the way anonymity can be: hot, ripe, and feeding on sugars or the way the sugars are, anonymous & ripe, hot for the picking-off—ripening, a sugared thing, a focused heat, a vigor; & like hotness is anonymous—*here sugar, here ripe-scene*—the way a bad thing can taste metallic, and the cold a friend of a friend, and steel the business of un-friendship, the way a surprise can be—or something planned—a dark écriture, the planning of a surprise or the surprise of a plan gone dark, like writing on the wall: surprised or no, it has all gone as if pre-planned—a "darkening" unsurprising in its euphemism, as if intended to point a finger—the gun was exploratory, another way of getting to no him

---

* From JM Ledgard's novel, *Submergence*

# The Arithmetic of Individuality Obscures the Much-Too-Young (Janet Napolitano Grieves)*

who can say how these things go? something in the water—a root consciousness—bubbling to the surface and we name you—the children—you were all much too young, & you must / we won't let the arithmetic define you—kiss of arithmetic for children so young—byebye, waved the mother & kissed you obscure—you were young, and to be young is to know that you must / we won't let obscurity define you—you were brave! competitive! & extremely kind—you were Taylor & Jessica & Joshua & Samantha—*hakuna matata* Daniel! *hakuna matata* Emily! spending time with your family was listed as your favorite thing to do—Brittany, who, Andrew, who now—all young and being brave now, Andrew who—we won't / you must have your own plan: being children won't do

---

* From an article on the UC Santa Barbara shootings in which Janet Napolitano, the University of California president and former secretary of homeland security, called the shooting an "unfathomable tragedy" and encouraged the crowd to remember and celebrate the unique qualities of each of the students who were killed. "All died much too young," Napolitano said. "It's important that we don't let the arithmetic of this tragedy define them. Their individuality should not be obscured."

Luke Baumgarten

# The Big Little City

Once upon a time, on a quiet Monday morning in a big little city near a torrentially roaring falls, citizens awoke with the power to summon forth the most jaw-dropping feats of sorcery.[1]

Well, eventually.

The power hadn't announced itself with thunder or clarions. It just floated in with the breeze and settled in the metaphysical spaces between bone and tendon, skin and sinew, and so we discovered the gift gradually, and in mundane ways. That first day, for example, Jeffrey Finer found himself craving a bagel and lox with his coffee when, *poof!*, a bagel with lox appeared. Elmore Franklin wished a little Bushmills into his Ovaltine and, similarly: *poof!* Protestant cocoa.

John Stockton, on increasingly rickety limbs, strode onto his personal basketball court for his 6 AM workout longing to once again snap off shots on twenty-year-old wrists. He sunk 759 free throws straight, a lifetime best, finally stopping not because he had missed, but because he'd forgotten to also long for youthful lungs.

Magic found its way into non-humans as well. Across town, a Boston Terrier named Corky mustered a preternatural burst of speed—as though ushered along by Hermes himself—finally catching the bastard tabby that roamed the alley behind his house.[2]

---

1   Including, but not limited to alchemy, augury, allurement, conjuration, necromancy and the odd diabolism.

2   Upon achieving this, his life's only clear goal, Corky became despondent, having no idea what to do next.

It took days, in fact, from those first spontaneous happenings for our exactly 209,525 citizens[3] to realize that what we thought were thoroughly private[4] and unique miracles was actually an entire city—for whatever reason, and by the grace of God-knows whom—beset by magic. It took Dan Kleckner spontaneously re-growing a mop of natural, luxurious hair[5] during the 6 o'clock news for us to really start putting it together.

As with any new skill, magic took time to master, and some were quicker on the uptake than others. Kleckner, in pollinating follicles long considered lost by Rogaine and Bosley alike, was an early prodigy. So too, a young boy named Davey. The child discovered, while playing in a puddle in his overgrown backyard on west Dean Avenue, that any action he performed with his Tonka truck was mimicked by the backhoes and dump trucks within eyesight over in the dirt lots of Kendall Yards. No fewer than 11 earthmovers of various sizes and tonnages were flung by invisible hand down the gorge and

---

3   The census-designated population of the big little city in question, representing all persons currently residing within its contiguous limits, most emphatically not including those persons residing in the county at large, not even those in the contentious, prickly suburbs outside the city but within the urban growth boundary.

4   I, for what its worth, had wished to God for one uneventful bowel movement before I died and, praise the Lord, was blessed to find that wish granted.

5   Looking not unlike his idol and secret crush, Mick Jones of Foreigner.

into the river before officials discovered the source of the mischief and replaced little Davey's trucks with a set of dinosaurs.[6]

*The New York Times'* Tim Egan, upon hearing of the boy from his brother Dan[7], wrote a column comparing (favorably) Davey's destructive mischief to those jurisdictions in the interior west which had failed to properly regulate coal trains, fracking, and the transport of highly flammable Bakken crude from the boomtowns of North Dakota to the shipping terminals of the Puget Sound.

"This adorable little boy is too young to understand the impact of his limitless power," Egan wrote, "but we, after a century of environmental havoc, we know the impact wrought by the lack of limits on big coal and big oil exactly."

The column did little to change national attitudes about extraction and consumption of fossil fuels, but it created considerable interest in the boy—whom the New York Post subsequently dubbed "Voodoo Doll Davey"—and curiosity about the big little city of his birth.

A wave of tourism followed and, once word spread it wasn't just little Davey with the power to reorient the cosmos, the city became the beneficiary of considerable in-migration. Some migrants hoped modestly to be healed by proximity to magic bearers. Others lusted to wield such power themselves.

The more ambitious of the speculators quickly discovered that their new powers enjoyed a global reach, so long as they stayed squarely within the city and had a clear sense—whether from crystalline memory or HD webcam—of their target abroad. Thus was Venice lifted onto sturdier mooring by a humanities professor originally from Provo, Utah.

The economic potential of staking a claim in what might become the world's leading and only magic-exporting region led predictably

---

6   Taking care to not include any mastodons or other ancient creatures previously endemic to the area, for fear their bones might spring joyously from bedrock, clattering and dancing along to the tune of the boy's play.

7   Tim, who had left the big little city for greener pastures, was not anointed with magic, but Dan, who had remained his entire life, was. Not wanting to be, in any way, compared to western regulators, Dan initially kept this fact from his brother.

to land grabbing. Interests based a world away—Qatar, Kamchatka, Kuala Lumpur—bought properties sight unseen, urging land values to heights rivaled only by teeming metropolises.

Such rapid explosion in demand troubled the big little city's leaders, pundits and literati. Officials didn't take action, though, until a pair of upstart developers based in Shenzen demolished a mansion of historical significance to put up a 20-story mixed-use[8] tower.

Mayor Camden and Council President Echart called a joint press conference and announced that, perhaps for the first time ever, they had agreed on a course of action, halting all new construction within city limits. The move was neither definitive nor final, they stressed. Just a cooling-off period.

The men shook hands as a symbol of this same-mindedness, but each squeezed ferociously, and with a hint of malice, as though thinking it a shame to let political consensus spoil an opportunity to inflict actual physical pain.[9]

In response, the County Commissioners—pro-development to the last and ravenous for new tax revenue—voted unanimously to expand the urban growth boundary, then circulated full-page ads in the Wall Street Journal, Financial Times, *Der Handelsblatt* and the Dubai Daily Bugle, inviting developers of all nationalities and predilections to follow their Chinese counterparts and build gigantic structures atop the region's thick bedrock—land that could be had, if they acted fast, for low, low prices. The trawl was embarrassingly successful, hauling in gulf-state sheiks, tech moguls from Mumbai, Russian oligarchs, Albertan tar-sand speculators[10], and the odd carpeted Trump.

Land values at the big little city's fringes briefly eclipsed that of the core, but the bullishness turned savage when the growth-bound-

---

8    The tower was to host an ambitious mix of residential, commercial and retail space—with both state of the art sport courts and a tasteful, yet hyper-modern funerary—and and be marketed as the world's first live/work/eat/play/die building.

9    The moment might have escaped notice, if not for an electric gust whipping up all loose paper and small personal effects in the room into a cyclone of pure human animus centered on the men.

10   Seeking to diversify their portfolios, obviously.

ary land was found to be devoid of any and all magicks. The Commissioners planned to simply ride out the furor, until a series of increasingly suggestive late-night "meetings" with the "attaché" of an unbending oligarch "persuaded" them to make certain the oligarch received the power he longed for.

This left the commissioners with a moral quandary. On one hand, what the oligarch wanted—an expansion of the city limits to include his large tract of acreage—was a virtual legal impossibility without the consent of the city council. On the other hand, breaking the law would allow them to keep their lives.

Being people of profound moral fiber, their unanimous first thought was that preserving the sanctity and honor of the office was a principle worth dying for. After a moment's discussion, though, the three realized that, blackmail or no, freeing up large tracts of land to commerce that had previously been shackled by excessive and Draconian regulation was an unalloyed good. Remaining unmolested by a certain gargantuan Cossack was a fortuitous and poetic consequence, of course, but that only underscored the Providential correctness of their cause.

For if it were a great honor to die for the sanctity of their office, they concluded with a clink of Chardonnay, even greater was the honor to live—*truly live!*—in service of the free market.[11]

The next afternoon, their heads unclouded by the fermented fruit of hasty ambition[12], they decided hocus pocus should be a last resort. First, they would besiege the city council—that haughty Leftist redoubt—with parliamentary procedure.

At the next city council meeting, Commissioners Malkin, McGinn and Paris, along with the local Home Builder's Association and representatives from a virtual United Nations of international landowners[13] came to the council with a plan they promised would

---

11  McGinn, in a moment of revelry, next said that if the plan worked, she might finally—after years of contemplating it—dye her hair blonde. Malkin replied, "Lady, if this works, I'll frost my tips!"

12  And also recognizing that only Commissioner Paris had a home within the magic zone, making him one county sorcerer against an city of thaumaturges.

13  Including, of course, our attaché.

bring both density and tax revenues to the outer edges of a newly expanded city limits while still keeping their building moratorium within the old limits in tact.

Paris, a man who relished these sorts of tense negotiations made the pitch.

The city would file to annex all land inside the current urban growth boundary, Paris explained, and the county would assent to an aid in any way possible. All the Commissioners asked, he said, was just enough of the new tax revenues to keep the county solvent.

The Council was surprisingly amenable. Councilman Travan declared his support straight away and both Councilman Fallon and Councilwoman Husht called the idea intriguing. Councilwoman Waldorf called it a cynical attempt to cash in on a man-made market bubble on the verge of bursting, but that reaction was to be expected from a goddamn Trotskyite. The real trick would be seeing where Echart and Schuyler landed. Though too liberal by half, Paris considered both to be the sort of men who grease the skids of their unalloyed ambition with a certain, pragmatism. Echart's ambition especially came close to rivaling his own, as did his willingness to come to the table when he smelled a feast. Paris guessed density and tax revenue would be one-two punches to their big government pleasure centers. Turning from Waldorf, Paris asked, "What do you think, gentlemen?"

"Well, you know I like density," Echart said in his folksy way.

"Yeah," Schuyler replied. "I love density. I think we all like density..." The councilman paused, and Paris, perhaps too intoxicated by his own argument, didn't recognize the feint. "But we'd need to think about roads."

"And transit," Echart agreed.

"Mhmmm," Schuyler again, "The denser you get, the more pedestrians you're going to have."

The men ping-ponged back and forth about the sort of infrastructure density requires, and how they wouldn't want to do anything that didn't first have a plan in place for complete streets at a minimum, and perhaps a light rail to the core, the airport and the tech parks on the eastern edge of the valley.

Commissioner Paris, a man who by his own admission does not suffer fools, felt a fire rising inside himself, stoked not just by this obstructionist double feature, or the way the other leftists on the council seemed to nod like bobble-heads, but also by the heat of the gaze a few rows back from the man who seemed capable of doing horrible, horrible things. He chewed his growing anger. Felt his face flushing.

Finally, both Echart and Schuyler agreed that, given the highly volatile nature of the city's newfound supernatural resource, neither would want to make any move for annexation until after conducting a lengthy review and planning process.

That proved to be the straw.

"You should be *begging* to annex this land!" Paris cried, launching into a lengthy rebuttal that referenced broadly—from Buckminster Fuller to Brutalism, Pyongyang to Potemkin—his multi-partite disdain for needlessly directing growth, especially when it meant cooling off what seemed, judging by this United Nations of developers behind him, that the whole world—"The whole goddamned world!"—was at their doorstep, begging to be let in.

*What right did any of us have to tell the rest of us what sort of neighborhoods to live in, Paris cried. Who are you, sirs and madams, but stewards who should open the door to future prosperity for our children and grandchildren?*

Fully flushed and panting now, he concluded, "You should be dying to annex this whole. Damned. *County!*" Bringing his hand down on the dias once, hard, for each of the last three words.

The crowd gasped. One person screamed.

The members of the council seemed confused. What had just happened? Paris, caught up in his moment, wasn't sure either. The gasp became a clamor, and one woman, her hand to her mouth, pointed with her other hand to the wall above the council. Fallon, Travan, Husht, Schuyler, Echart and Waldorf all turned to look at the stylized and somewhat homely map in enamel of the big little city that had hung above the council chamber the mid 1970s. Paris looked up as well. The city's three council districts—each portrayed in hues of greenish blue and bluish green, and nestled quaintly on a much larger field of white representing the county—had grown, in spectacular fashion, judging by the gasps, to encompass the entire county, just as Paris had imagined. The enamel, warped by witchcraft into a bulbous mass, seemed ready to spill the bounds of the county line.

Echart turned to Paris and Paris saw a raw and familiar anger. Paris took a step back, feeling an unfavorable corner had been turned.[14]

Quickly after, Schuyler and Waldorf wheeled on Paris as well. The Commissioner looked back at the Russian, who wore an expression of confusion and menace. Had this American just won the day or sunk the whole endeavor?

Trying to assess the situation quickly while chaos still reigned, Paris looked next to Malkin. The man's face showed he was only beginning to grasp what had happened.

Paris spun around to look at McGinn. He gasped. Her hair. Her hair—a deep chestnut—as long as he had known her—now glowed flaxen.

Paris looked back to Malkin, and upon seeing that he wore the hair of a late-century rap rocker, the weight of what was happening nearly brought Paris to his knees. The man's passion hadn't just changed a map, it had redrawn reality.

Echart saw it a second later. "McGinn went blonde!" he yelled. "Roll it back!"

Paris, understanding, at last, that there would be no diplomatic solution, yelled to his cohort: "To arms, you fools!"

Much of the next 10 minutes in the council chambers is lost to history.[15] What we've gathered is mostly inference from outside the

---

14   It's important to note that Paris had been the subject, just weeks earlier, of a lengthy profile in the local weekly paper where his decades of public service were discussed in the most polarized terms. The article began with four on-the-record quotes: **"One of the most effective politicians I've ever worked with,"** says a current city councilman. **"He likes to bully people,"** says the mayor of Airway Heights. **"He is one of the brightest political brains we've ever had in this city,"** a former city councilwoman says. **"He's the worst individual I ever met,"** a former city council president says. **"This son of a bitch caused me six years of misery."**

15   Whether because of mass magic- or trauma-induced amnesia, a tontine of deception or a mix of the two.

chamber[16], pieced together from accounts of magical powers gained and lost all over the county.

At around 7 pm, for example, roughly an hour into the meeting, a retired Air Force Crew Chief named Duane Renz, in the sleepy exurb of Country Homes, lost in a moment of wistful reminiscence, found himself willing into re-existence his wife, a fiercely spirited woman who went by the name "Mickey" in life and would have killed you for using her given name, Maxine. In the time the Battle of the Council and Commission raged, a period of between 10 and 15 minutes, Mickey fussed with Duane's shirt, bummed a cigarette, offered him lunch, and criticized the way he'd kept up the cleaning, before finally taking to the walls, floors and ceiling with scrub bucket and hand sponge, the way she had every day for 54 years.

When the tide of battle turned decisively away from the out-numbered Commissioners, Maxine blinked, unceremoniously, out of existence again.

A tense and quiet stalemate has followed that battle. It seems clear this new power will fundamentally shift something deep within us. And though we are learning, every day, wondrous and troubling things, it feels at times as though the shift has already come. Also abundantly clear: this power—like all other powers yet known—has limits circumscribed by the immensity of our love and the narrow-ness of our vision.

Upon hearing his grandfather's story, Duane's grandson, who lives on the city's south hill, was deeply moved, and offered to try and make his grandmother's return permanent. The young man had practically grown up with them, and would be able to sketch her well, but after a long moment of reflection, Duane declined. He told his grandson he feared the woman his grandson brought back would have only the wry, doting manner she brought to childrearing and not the full fire she reserved for her husband in his more human moments. That woman had given him a lifetime of grief to go along

---

16    Witnesses within the chamber who say anything at all remember Councilman Travan—far to the right of everyone in the room and most everyone on the planet—nonetheless saw Paris's witching as tantamount to war. He reportedly yelled, "*Sic semper tyrannis!*" and jumped in on the side of the council.

with a lifetime of companionship, Duane reasoned, and he couldn't bear the thought of having one version of her, but not the other.

The grandson next asked if Duane would like to come live with his fiancée and he for a while, so that he could bring her back whole. That wouldn't do either, the grandfather said. "I appreciate the offer, Lukey. I just hate the shit out of that South Hill."

Anastasia Hilton

# Free-Range Kids

All around The Ridge at Hamblen, our children were disappearing. By ones and twos they would go, plucked from their play by some unknown force. The scenes were hideous: an empty sandbox, a purple Barney shovel lying forsaken on the grass nearby; or good Mrs. Johnson clutching a plate of warm cookies, calling, "Suuu-sie! Suu-sie! Susie?" in a driveway strewn with side-walk chalk. Such uncertainty bred fear in us unlike anything we'd ever known; someone was snatching the children without leaving a clue as to his method or, worse, intent. And so, in the days and years that followed this treachery, we shuttered the windows and arranged our children's days so that we might keep an eye on them at all times. Scabby-kneed, in-at-dark neighborhood exploration gave way to organized sports, violin lessons, and total immersion French language playdates. In the process of keeping our little ones from harm, we discovered a new aim: concerted cultivation, as they're calling it these days. We use all of those safe, structured hours to foster our children's every glimmer of talent. Perhaps our little ones' trophies and ribbons help assuage our guilt for taking their freedom, as some of the more flippant fathers claim, but if such is the case, so be it. What choice do we have?

I say "we" as if I were one of the fortunate mothers who had been in time to shutter her home against that tricky snatcher of youths. If only it were so! But no, I was one of the tortured ones. It will be my lifelong regret that my two dear babes were among the first to go, tricked by a man cloaked in the threads of propriety. I have spent these decades in remorse and longing for the precious children I allowed to slip from my embrace, and although I have been luckier than some (my children, after many years, returned to me, albeit changed in unconscionable ways), I know the importance of vigilance.

And now, I have discovered, a backlash is rising against our efforts. A group of regrettable mothers has organized, fools who claim to celebrate the children's "freedom" to go unattended once again, to promote the habits of those carefree days before the snatcher came. "We have joined a national movement advocating our children's liberation. Let them wander, explore, and (gasp!) learn from their mistakes," their website pronounces. Just this morning, the originator of the Free-Range Kids movement appeared, smiling into the *Good Morning, America* cameras. "Our children need us, yes!" she cried to an enthusiastic Brooklyn mommy crowd. "They need us *to leave them alone!* They need us *to step out of the way!* So mamas, put those kids on the subway with a kiss and a map, and *stop worrying!*"

How can they ignore the great peril? Don't they grapple with uncertainty every time their children are loosed from their loving grip, perhaps for the last time? But we all felt that ease once. There was a time when everyone in our lovely little Spokane exurb had fallen under a spell of complicity. We all ignored the danger until our weakness opened a crack in the world.

My girl, Annabelle, was on the cusp of pubescence the year of her disappearance, a gentle spirit with strawberry cheeks and eyes a deep evening-sky blue. But in the weeks that led to her undoing, a maelstrom brewed in her. I have lived with regret for not seeing the signs, but what tween doesn't cultivate that kind of angst? Locked in her room (Do Not Disturb!), her stereo's disconsolate melodies drowning and reviving her by the hour, she appeared a perfectly appropriate twelve-year-old.

I had resigned myself to patiently riding out the years of her adolescence, delighting for the time in the development of her brother, Dirk, who at nine was promising to grow into as fine a man as his dear father had been. Among his friends he was a natural leader, quick-witted and always the ablest with a skateboard or Hacky Sack. He kept three charming rats, Wynken, Blynken, and Nod, whom he taught to perform delightful tricks like roll the barrel and dunk the basketball. Dirk had spent much of his childhood in Annabelle's shadow, content to let her direct their play, but as she shut herself away from us, he came into his own. It was a pleasure for me to witness. But how criminal that I didn't see the signs, didn't understand that change—any change—brought us instability and made the children hungry for the bait the snatcher laid.

We had a certain dog-catcher in Hamblen—Titus was his name— of whom Dirk and some of the other children had grown quite fond. When Titus's truck appeared, they would bound outside and follow behind him. This new development didn't sit well with me, but I was hesitant to interfere. After all, Dirk was a fatherless boy, and these events occurred in the days before the first disappearances. If anything, my concern lay more in Dirk's abandonment of his goal of becoming President in favor of driving a dog-catcher's truck.

The other adults of Hamblen didn't share in the children's enthusiasm either, due to Titus's habit of rounding up every hound that dared to step outside. License, collar, tags—these were nothing to him. One glimpse of a wagging tail from behind a house, and Titus would lure the pup with his irresistible whistle—an instrument that, in addition, piqued the interest of every neighborhood animal from pet to wild beast. Moose descended from the wooded hills, cats rose up from their sunny naps and yowled into the air; even Wynken, Blynken, and Nod rattled their cage in fits of desire. This racket, and the nuisance of having to retrieve every Fido and Fifi from the pound, caused the neighborhood to cast aspersions on Titus, and after the president of the homeowners association's collie disappeared, we drew up a petition. The dog-catcher was fired.

That summer brought the arrival of Charlie, a new ice-cream man. From the beginning, something about him alarmed me. I admit now that I made quite a scene about his presence in the neighborhood. However, in my defense, he came out of nowhere just about the time the first children disappeared: first Timmy, and then Suzie, and then little Leigh Wilkerson, who vanished from Hamblen Park. Whenever I heard the dizzying chime of his truck at the end of the block, I would shudder as the kids' excitement grew to manic levels. What was it—*is* it—about those trucks that renders all children helpless? I tried to no avail to keep my children from him, enticing them with my triple banana splits and labor-intensive sundaes, but my offers fell flat next to the ridiculous power of a Bomb Pop or Nutty Buddy.

Certainly, it was not just the ice-cream, for not only had Dirk become as enamored with Charlie as he had been with Titus, Annabelle had become fond, as well. In her I sensed a longing beyond Dirk's, and I grew more fearful by the day. I remember clearly the afternoon when she ran through the front door, licking the side of an ice-cream sandwich, giggling nonstop—not about ice-cream, but about Charlie. "He's so *crazy!*" she squealed, to which Dirk, tight-lipped, replied, "No, he's not. He's cool." A dreamy-eyed Annabelle corrected him. "No, I meant in a *good* way. Crazy good, like *awesome*."

And so, soon came the last day I would see my children until they returned to me years later, the vestiges of childhood stripped away, their lives altered beyond repair. In an effort to avoid this fate, I forbade them to visit the truck unless I followed closely at their heels. This rule sent Annabelle into fits of sullen pouting. She insisted I buy my own treat, telling me, "Look natural, Mom, like you're totally just there for ice-cream, and, like, *please* don't talk to me." I kept to this contract but maintained a close eye on the two of them, glowering at Charlie as my Push-Up melted in its cylinder.

One such day, as we stood by the jingling truck, Judy Parks emerged from her house and waved me over. "Have you heard?" She whispered. "A boy who lives on Pinecrest. Yesterday morning." I glared at Charlie through the back door of his truck. He sat golden-eyed and grinning with his feet propped up on a freezer while the neighborhood children ogled his wares. "I don't trust that man," I told her. "Who? *Charlie?*" she laughed. "Why, he wouldn't harm a mouse." Annabelle flipped her hair between her fingers and absentmindedly pulled her flip-flop on, off, on, off as Charlie whispered some story that captivated her attention. Dirk kicked his Hacky

Sack in a circle of friends, but glanced in the truck's window as if he were performing his kicks to impress. I felt already the loss I have known every day for these years since, the awful sense of my children slipping away, over the ridge of my heart toward a distant, unknown land.

I have tried in vain to recollect with any clarity the hours that followed that moment. My grave suspicion is that Charlie sold me an enchanted Push-Up, for I lay feverish on the couch with the TV on, dreaming of a land with sparrows brighter than peacocks and horses with eagles' wings. Interwoven with a rerun of *Judge Judy*, it was indeed a most curious trance. I awoke to a furious rattle of the rats' cage to find the front door wide open, the children long gone, and the street empty but for a dirty Bomb Pop wrapper blowing end over end down the sidewalk.

In my mourning for Annabelle and Dirk, I succumbed to insomnia, often staying awake for days on end. Through it I came to possess a clarity of mind that told me what none of us had been able to see—Titus and Charlie were one and the same. The signs were unmistakable: the odd and tinny quality of both voices, the golden glitter of the eyes, and even the chain around Charlie's neck that, although it disappeared beneath his collar, must have held the very whistle Titus had possessed. Even now, I surmised, it was his music that contained the magic. It tinkled merrily from a loudspeaker atop his truck, a literal siren song that lured the children to him so that he might have his pick. The lyrics themselves seemed designed to taunt the mothers as he drew their babes into his world: *Sailing, sailing over the bounding main, where many a stormy wind shall blow 'ere Jack comes home again...*

The neighbors all thought me crazy, as I never offered proof enough to satisfy them. I suppose their concern was understandable; after all, good Mrs. Johnson formed the ridiculous theory that all the children had been subjected to the Amphibian Curse. The poor dear went about gathering up every toad in the neighborhood looking for signs of whose lost child might be trapped within. For most, however, the disappearances signaled the coming of an outsider, the blank-faced silhouette of a man that would become the universal symbol of Stranger Danger. For me, it was obvious: we were under the spell of a monster.

"It's he," I insisted. "It's Charlie, but you'll only see when it's too late for you." I stopped short of telling them that Charlie and Titus were one; they were already in such disagreement with me, I knew I would lose their faith entirely. Regrettably, in a moment of candor I told Judy, who in turn told them all. They offered me condoling shoulder rubs and glanced at one another in pity. "Dear," said June McAllister, "Titus lives in town. He works at the Northwest Boulevard Subway. He sold me a Cold Cut Combo just the other day."

As the days went by I found my friendships replaced by solemn whispers and, eventually, benign neglect. They would never understand—which is why I believe his magic was very strong—that Titus's appearance in town meant nothing, and that Charlie's continued presence in the neighborhood spelled doom for more of our children. Even some mothers who'd lost children thought me mad, so when I flew out my front door and attacked Charlie one hot afternoon, they threatened to send me to the state hospital. After that I kept to myself and spent my days with Wynken, Blynken, and Nod.

And so more children disappeared, and more parents lost their faith, until at last our kids were kept in sight and their activities tightly supervised. I have been satisfied with this change in the tide; Hamblen mothers today are happier for it and rarely lose their children the way we did. This is why we must remain alert, for the words "free range" probably drip from the mouth of the snatcher like syrup already. It is no coincidence that Charlie disappeared over the ridge for good that summer. Now the disappearances come into our living rooms by way of the six o'clock news.

The neighborhood houses emptied out and refilled over the years until I was the last original homeowner to remain. I enjoyed the young families and allowed my delight in their children to sit in the lap of my heart's pain. I had long since given up hope of ever seeing Annabelle and Dirk again when, one day, tending to my small garden plot behind the house, I glimpsed a most unusual sight on the ridge. A young man crested the hill, along with a living, moving tree, which at first I thought he carried, but soon realized walked independent of him. As they drew nearer, I recognized them as my beloved children grown to adulthood. Dirk was not at all as I would have expected; his father's hardiness had emptied from him, and what remained was a scraggly waif clad in silver studded jeans and a distressed Black Sabbath T-shirt. Annabelle was all branches and leaves, her root legs heavy as if from a journey of a thousand miles. Her sweet spirit was still perceptible, but two disquieting knot holes formed her eyes and made me look away. Still, our reunion had come at last, and we embraced and cried for the wonder and absurdity of it all. "Tell me this one thing," I implored. "Was it *he?*" Dirk shrugged and fingered his rattail braid. "Uh…yeah," he said. "Sorry. Anyways, we're, like, not supposed to talk about it."

With a swish, swish of leaves, Annabelle turned and walked away from us, her heavy root limbs lumbering up the small hill behind the house. She slid her roots deep into the soil of our home, where she remains today, growing red, ripe apples by the armloads and shading my kitchen window from the sun. Dirk stayed on for some years, but never recovered the quickness and enthusiasm of his youth. Most of his days were spent lying on the sofa eating Cheetos and watching reruns of Gilligan's Island. As any mother would, I encouraged him to register at Spokane Falls or join a Meetup, but he clutched the remote and slid further down the cushion. Then one morning, just like that, he bounded off the couch and headed for Pullman, where he took a job as a chimney sweep. These days he plays the flute in a Jethro Tull cover band and has a girlfriend who, although a bit of a troll, seems to make him happy.

As I approach the winter of my life, I have come to accept that I will never witness the future I would have wanted for my children, especially Annabelle. What devastation those stolen years wrought will forever remain beyond my knowing. As the neighborhood children play in her branches and the heady scent of spiced apple pie drifts out the window, I can only hope she senses how much her mother loves her. So to these mothers, these adherents of the so-called Free Range Kids movement, I say this: these dangers are real, and they will slip in in the midst of your inattention to change your destiny forever. It is only our vigilance that keeps the snatcher from this land. We must be careful, so careful, so careful.

Leah Sottile

# Burn

The caterpillar felt sick as he inched away from the misty glen where the little girl in the blue dress and the frilly smock now sat, looking confused.

He'd done a lot of things he wasn't proud of—but this? He felt downright shitty about telling the kid to eat the mushroom. *One side will make you larger! One side will make you smaller!* He'd reached a new low.

He just wished he could inch away quicker so he didn't have to hear the drugs hit the poor kid. You'd think sixteen legs would be good for something.

Truth was, the girl caught him off guard. She was the first he'd seen come through the forest in all the time he'd been directing traffic from the mushroom.

All day he'd send the good folks toward the Cheshire Cat's tree—guys like Humpty Dumpty who used herb to nurse his pain and ex-Cards who didn't have to worry about drug testing now that they were retired.

The shifty methheads—he'd send them toward Hatter's place. For his services, the Cat hooked him up with a bag whenever he needed one and never went light on the skunky green buds. He felt grateful that the Cat believed in him when no one else did. It helped the Caterpillar keep his dark side in the shadows.

After he'd escaped the genocide, when that terrible drunken beast had invaded the garden and thoughtlessly plucked the legs off of everyone he loved, squished his family without remorse, the Caterpillar—the last of his kind—spun out of control.

He took to hanging out with Hatter and the mangy hare at those tea parties that never seemed to end. It made him sick to his stomach to think about how he used to take a bump when he woke in Hatter's rickety shack, drop crystal into his morning tea and spend days trying to perform surgery on the doormouse—who they'd left inside the teapot for two weeks and starved to death. The stench when they pulled him out of there...

The Cat was always telling him never to forget the anger of watching his loved ones die, that his rage was his salvation. But these days the Caterpillar did everything he could to tune that idea out. Day after day, he'd lay across the mushroom's pillowy top, loading fat hookah bowls mixed with molasses shisha, blowing smoke rings into the sky and telling the flowers in the garden how beautiful they were. Maybe he was a dirty old man, but he could have sworn those young roses were wearing fewer petals lately. Better a dirty old man than an angry one, he figured.

When he'd inched a good twenty feet, the old Caterpillar reached the base of the creaky weeping willow, and gave one of the long branches a hard tug. Way up at the top, he could see the cat, grinning as he weighed out buds onto a scale.

"Hey, man," the Cheshire Cat yelled down from the tree. "What the fuck was up with that kid? *Tell* me you sent her to Hatter's place." He carefully made his way down from the branches, which the Caterpillar thought was funny considering the Cat's teleportation skills.

"Are you kidding? Send a kid toward that tweaker?" the Caterpillar said. "He'd have her sold into the sex trade in an hour. I can't have that shit on my conscience."

The cat shrugged.

"No man, I told her to eat the mushroom. It'll fuck her up, but I figure that thing's ancient enough that it won't freak her out too bad," the Caterpillar said, patting the pockets of his sixteen pairs of pants. "You got a smoke?"

"Tough choices, man. Tough choices," the Cat said, drawing a cigarette out of thin air and lighting it with his claw. He had so many weird party tricks. "Anyway, a stoned kid's the least of our worries."

The Caterpillar took a drag and coughed. "Worries?"

"Come on, I'll show you." The Cat lowered his neck so the Caterpillar could inch up onto his striped fur. "Hold tight."

The Cat hunched his body and skittered low under the brush. The Caterpillar could tell they were heading toward the Queen's palace.

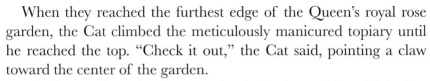

When they reached the furthest edge of the Queen's royal rose garden, the Cat climbed the meticulously manicured topiary until he reached the top. "Check it out," the Cat said, pointing a claw toward the center of the garden.

The Caterpillar didn't even need to look—he could smell it before his eyes could see it.

Right in the middle of the Queen's garden sat a brand new building. GREEN QUEEN the sign read, "Your royal marijuana shoppe." The Caterpillar's jaw dropped.

"That bitch fucking legalized," the Cat said, sticking a cigarette in his teeth, and producing another smaller one for the caterpillar.

A line of customers stretched far outside the store, down the garden aisles. It twisted and wound its way in and out and in and out until it faded into the distance. Around the castle, the gardens of roses had been replaced with long, tall rows of marijuana plants. The armies of cards had traded their spears for gardening shears, and were hunched over the plants, clipping, watering, fertilizing.

The Caterpillar could make out the faces of the Cheshire Cat's most loyal customers in the crowd: the White Queen, the Dodo Bird, the Mock Turtle.

"What the hell, man?" The Caterpillar gaped. "Is that Tweedle Dee and Tweedle Dum!"

"Yeah, dude, but fuck them. I hated having those guys up into the tree. They'd always forget their cash and would end up fighting over some childish BS—the Queen can have them," the Cat said, exhaling a thin stream of smoke.

The Caterpillar's eyes scanned the long, twisting queue, trying to tune out the terrible bleating of the White Rabbit—whose fur was matted into dreadlocks and was now fronting some terrible reggae band stationed at the front of the shop.

"It's not the legal dope I'm worried about," the Cat said. "The novelty of paying 50 hedgehogs for what I sell for 20 will wear off. It's him I'm worried about."

The Caterpillar followed the Cheshire Cat's gaze until it met the green scaly back of the one beast he'd never thought he'd see again. It felt like someone had stepped onto old Caterpillar's chest.

The devil was walking among them. He couldn't believe that it was legal marijuana that would bring the Jabberwocky out of hiding.

He'd been waiting what felt like his whole life to face off with the beast, preparing for years for one last go-round—for one final romp with the beautiful, red rage deep inside of him. The Cheshire Cat had been urging him not to be a zenned-out pothead, but to remember the anger that made him who he was. The only reason the Caterpillar had lived for so long was because his heart wanted revenge.

"I'll teleport you back to the tree," the Cheshire Cat said. "You be ready."

The Caterpillar inched as high as he could up the old willow tree before his lungs felt like they were about to catch fire.

As he climbed, he thought about what he would say. How it would go down. The Cheshire Cat had always said that when the time came, he'd know exactly what to do. *Trust the angry gift inside of you, follow the dark white light wherever it leads you.*

He couldn't have reached the lowest branch sooner before he could hear the Jabberwocky crashing through the brush. "Catch up, Jab—I don't think she'll wait long," the Cat called back over his shoulder as he ran.

"You better not be yanking my chain, Cat," the Jabberwocky roared. "If I lost my place in line for nothing, you'd better hook me up with a twenty sack for free."

"I'm tellin you, man!" the Cat said as he reached the tree. The Jabberwocky lumbered out from the bushes, his back to the willow. His eyes darted around the clearing, nostrils sniffing the air for a whiff of anything female.

The Caterpillar's chest was heaving now. He was panting, heart thumping, blood seething hot in his veins. He looked down at his rows of legs, and saw tiny curls of steam rising from the surface of his skin. And he wasn't blue anymore, but a deep, dark shade of crimson red.

"I don't see any chicks, man" the Jabberwocky spat at the Cat, whose grin was now wider and scarier than ever. The beast backed up, his wings almost touching the willow now.

The Cheshire Cat laughed—a high cackle, almost a squeal. With one long, glimmering claw the Cat pointed over the Jabberwocky's shoulder.

"You're right, there's no chicks here," the Cat yelled. "But go ahead and say hello to my little friend, you scaly son of a bitch!"

The Jabberwocky whipped around just in time to see the old Caterpillar, so red he was almost black now, wriggling out of his wrinkly blue skin.

The beast went pale.

The Caterpillar was rising above the earth as his gaze locked onto the wet orange eyes of his foe. He felt air under his legs, felt the world bend suddenly at his will. All around him, the forest floor was on fire.

There he was hovering above the Earth, a giant, black winged butterfly, an old man reborn. The anger of the ages burning in his heart.

"It's time, old man!" the Cat yelled from below.

The Caterpillar took one breath—the deepest, clearest breath he'd ever taken in his entire life. And when he exhaled, out came an inferno of black flames. His giant wings stirred the wind, food for the fire.

All he could feel was the beautiful power of his rage. And all he could hear were screams. And all he could see was the skeleton of the Jabberwocky, dissolving into ashes.

And then the Caterpillar's wings were aflame, too, and rapture was finally his.

Kris Dinnison

# Honey and Patience

When Father brought Bearskin home, my sisters were disappointed to say the least.

Prima ran screaming into our bedroom like the devil was chasing her. She slammed the door and threw the bolt. Then she laughed her ass off.

I pressed my back against the wall, wondering if she'd finally lost it.

Prima rolled her eyes. "The oldest one always has to marry the stranger," she explained. "And there's no way I'm marrying that rank hairball Dad just brought home."

I pushed away from the wall, unbolted the door, and reached the parlor just in time to hear my other sister, Dila, berating the poor guy for his grooming.

"If it was just the hair, we could deal with it. A day at the salon for a full body wax, and we're good to go. But Jesus, I've run into actual bears who dressed better and smelled better than you." She waved her hand in front of her face. "Sorry, I'm going to have to pass."

"Father," I interrupted. "Can I get you and your friend something to drink?"

Father nodded, looking relieved.

"Suck up!" Dila spit at me as I pushed past her into the kitchen. I ignored her as I pulled Father's best bottle of Bourbon out of the high cupboard.

When I returned to the parlor, arms full of a strange assortment of food and drink, Father was thanking Bearskin for saving his life. By this he meant the stranger had given him a big sack of money, money which came endlessly from the pockets of Bearskin's coat. I call him Bearskin because he was wearing one. He gave no other name. His hair had grown so long everywhere that it was hard to tell the bear pelt from his own skin and hair.

"Have a drink with us, Tria." My father poured bourbon into two juice glasses as I fetched a third from the cupboard. "A toast." He raised his glass. "To good fortune and promises kept."

Bearskin's eyes filled with gratitude that made me think he hadn't known much kindness.

By the end of the night I had agreed to marry Bearskin. Our poor father, who misunderstood the women in his life so completely, thought I was making a great sacrifice. But this stranger was the longed-for escape from the thicket of thorns my life had become since mother died. Besides, after a couple of whiskeys and an evening of his stories, I was half in love with the guy, matted fur and all.

Before he left the next morning, he made it clear he'd be back in three years or not at all. He stood close. My body warmed as I breathed in his scent. Bearskin kissed my hand, and I loved the feel of his coarse hair on my fingers. He broke a ring in two and gave one half to me, which I put on a chain and tucked under my clothes so that my sisters wouldn't see it.

They were merciless after he left.

"He's going to kiss you with that filthy bear mouth. All kinds of nasty in there, I'd guess." Prima said.

"Just watch out for those claws on your wedding night." Dila pinched her face together. It seemed she couldn't even think about sex without making that face.

I never said anything, never responded. I just felt the cool curve and weight of the ring on my skin and willed him to return. I stopped cutting my hair, let it grow past my knees, let it fill my armpits and cover my legs. My father didn't seem to notice, but it put my sisters on edge.

"At least shave your pits," Prima pleaded. "It's mortifying, honestly!"

Dila left razors on my pillow, but lacked the courage to ask me to use them.

At night, when my sisters slept, I stroked the golden ring.

If my sisters were disappointed when Bearskin came back, they didn't show it. They didn't recognize him now that he wore a uniform instead of pelts, now that he was clean and shaved and handsome. But I knew right away. They served him wine before running to their rooms to deck themselves out in dresses that showed their ample cleavage and creamy skin.

I watched Bearskin, hiding behind the curtain of my hair, and waited for him to show me a sign that he knew me, that he still wanted me, that he was back to keep his promise. He approached me, digging in the pocket of his coat. As he pulled out his half of the the split ring. I drew the chain from my shirt, holding my half to his.

Then Bearskin smiled and kissed my hand. I missed the feel of his fur on my knuckles, but his nearness revealed the musk he carried before was his own. I leaned my face into his palm as he caressed and smoothed my tangles and told me I was beautiful.

My sisters emerged perfumed and painted just as Bearskin kissed me for the first time. He tasted of honey and berries and patience.

# Acknowledgements

I have quite a few people to thank for assistance with this book, particularly Keely Honeywell, who went above and beyond in designing and arranging the book's contents and exterior. This book would have been a fairy tale and nothing more if it weren't for Keely's focused magic. For the beautiful cover design, thank you to Karli Ingersoll; who is a generous, talented, and brilliant soul. Thank you to all of the writers in the book for entertaining such a tight deadline, and for suffering through edits, which, at times, were a bit rushed and frantic (apologies for my rabidity in such cases). Thank you to Russ Davis with Gray Dog Press for answering my inquiries about the book printing process. Thank you, too, to Kevin Taylor, who answered a lot of questions about how to go about accomplishing this book, and whose rad anthology of local writing, *Spokane Shorties*, is a must-buy for any bibliophile living in the area. And thank you to the many authors who generously offered to help edit the book.

If you missed seeing/hearing several of our authors read at the Lilac City Fairy Tales event at the Bing, then you also missed out on hearing incredible music from Liz Rognes and Mama Doll. Never fear! You can hear their music online and buy CDs at www.lizrognes.com and www.mamadollmusic. com. You can also stream Mama Doll's new album online at www.mamadoll.bandcamp.com.

And thank you to Jerry and Patty Dicker and The Friends of the Bing for inviting me to organize such a wild event, and for helping to fund the printing of these tales and poems.

I'm so delighted that proceeds from sales, after printing costs, etc., will go to support INK Spokane, Spokane Public Libraries, and the Spokane County Library District. These organizations enhance literacy and arts education for a spectacularly diverse public. It's wonderful to support them in this admittedly small way, because they support our communities immeasurably.

Gratefully,

Sharma Shields

# Bios

**Zan Agzigian**'s collection of poetry, *Stamen and Whirlwind*, was published by Gribble Press. She holds an MFA from EWU and lives in Spokane where she produces/hosts Soundspace for Spokane Public Radio.

**Luke Baumgarten** has been writing since he asked to borrow his father's legal pad and quilled a report about the revolutionary war in pre-school. Since then, he's written for *Spin*, *Billboard* and *Willamette Week*, in addition to an 8-year writing and editing hitch at *The Inlander*. He is a co-founder of Terrain, the founder of Fellow Coworking, and is currently serving as the Interim Executive Director of the Spokane Arts Fund.

**Sheri Boggs** is the Youth Collection Development Librarian for the Spokane County Library District. She's worked as a bookseller, librarian, editor and writer, and currently spins stories from her 1940s era house on the South Hill.

**Polly Buckingham**'s chapbook, *A Year of Silence*, won Jeanne Leiby Memorial Chapbook Award for Fiction. A recipient of a 2014 Washington State Artist Trust Fellowship, Polly teaches creative writing and literature at Eastern Washington University and is founding editor of *StringTown Press*. Her stories and poems appear or are forthcoming in *The Threepenny Review*, *The New Orleans Review*, *The North American Review*, and *The Moth*.

**Ann M. Colford** is a writer, editor, and occasional accountant, based in Spokane.

**Beth Cooley** has published poetry, essays and fiction, including two YA novels. She teaches writing and literature at Gonzaga University.

# **Bios** continued

Formerly a teacher and librarian, **Kris Dinnison** is now a writer and small business owner living in Spokane, Washington. Her first novel, *You and Me and Him*, comes out from Houghton Mifflin Harcourt in July 2015.

**Tim Greenup** teaches at Spokane Falls Community College. His poems have appeared in *Redivider, Leveler, interrupture,* and elsewhere.

**Kelly Milner Halls** has published more than 1000 articles and reviews, 40 nonfiction books for young readers, a YA anthology for older readers and this quirky story for the young at heart. Three short novels for middle grade readers will soon follow.

**Kerry Halls** lives with her boyfriend in a house where cats outnumber people 2.5 to 1. Having worked for independent businesses in the heart of downtown Spokane for most of her adult life, she has learned to appreciate the magic in the mundane, the weird, the desperate, and the dirty—a magic that informs her fiction.

**Anastasia Hilton** is an MFA candidate at the Inland Northwest Center for Writers, and fiction editor of Willow Springs. A Southern transplant, she now lives in Spokane with her husband and two daughters.

**Bruce Holbert** is the author of two novels, *Lonesome Animals* and *The Hour of Lead*, both published by Counterpoint Press.

# **Bios** continued

**Keely Honeywell** founded the literary magazine *RiverLit*. She also works as a designer and developer at Seven2.

**Melissa Huggins** is the director of Get Lit! Programs, a literary nonprofit that hosts an annual literary festival as well as creative writing programs for K-12 students. She received an MFA from Eastern Washington University and is currently at work on a novel. Her interviews with writers such as Joyce Carol Oates and William T. Vollmann have appeared in *Willow Springs*, and she is a contributor to thebarking.com.

**Samuel Ligon** is the author of a novel, *Safe in Heaven Dead*, and a book of stories, *Drift and Swerve*. He teaches at Eastern Washington University, and is the editor of *Willow Springs*.

**Brooke Matson**'s collection of poetry, *The Moons*, was published by Blue Begonia Press in 2012. Her poetry has also been published in *Weathered Pages*, (Blue Begonia Press, 2005), and various issues of *RiverLit*, for which she is currently the 2014 Poet in Residence.

**Simeon Mills** is a graphic novelist and writer. His work has appeared in *StringTown*, *The Boiler Journal*, *Monkey Bicycle*, *RiverLit*, and elsewhere. His graphic novel, *Easy Reader*, received a 2012 Artist Trust grant.

**Shann Ray** is the author of *American Masculine*, winner of the American Book Award, the High Plains Book Award, and the Bakeless Prize. He is also the author of *Forgiveness and Power in the Age of Atrocity*, a work of creative nonfiction political theory, and Balefire, a collection of poems.

# Bios continued

**Laura Read** has published poems in a variety of journals, most recently in *Alaska Quarterly Review* and *New Madrid*. Her chapbook, *The Chewbacca on Hollywood Boulevard Reminds Me of You*, was the 2010 winner of the Floating Bridge Chapbook Award, and her collection, *Instructions for My Mother's Funeral*, was the 2011 winner of the AWP Donald Hall Prize for Poetry and was published in 2012 by the University of Pittsburgh Press. She teaches English at Spokane Falls Community College and lives in Spokane with her husband Brad and their two sons, Benjamin and Matthew.

**Marianne Salina** is a writer in Spokane and received her MFA from Eastern Washington University. Her short stories appear in *The Adirondack Review*, *Split Lip Magazine*, *Birkensnake*, and various other online publications. An English teacher at the community colleges for several years, Marianne currently works at Gonzaga University.

**Nicole Sheets** teaches at Whitworth University. Her essays have appeared in *Mid-American Review*, *Image*, *Hotel Amerika*, *Tampa Review*, and other journals. She's the web editor for *Rock & Sling*, and the editor of a forthcoming online anthology of nonfiction about church camp.

**Sharma Shields** is the author of the *Favorite Monster: Stories*, winner of the Autumn House Fiction Prize. Her debut novel, *The Sasquatch Hunter's Almanac*, will be published by Henry Holt in early 2015.

**Kathryn Smith** has an MFA in creative writing from Eastern Washington University. Recent poems have appeared or are forthcoming in *Rock & Sling*, *The Cresset*, *Floating Bridge Review* and *River-Lit*, as well as the anthology Spokane Shorties.

# **Bios** continued

**Leah Sottile** is a Spokane-based fiction writer and freelance journalist. Her work has been featured by *Al Jazeera America*, *The Atlantic*, *Seattle Weekly*, *Medium* and *Decibel*, among others. A fan of graphic novels and punk rock, she wrote her first comic for the 2013 Comic Book Legal Defense Fund's Liberty Annual on freedom of speech issues.

**Rachel Toor** teaches in the MFA program at Eastern Washington University. Her most recent book, a novel, is *On the Road to Find Out* published in 2014 by Farrar Straus and Giroux.

Award-winning writer **Nance Van Winckel** had two new books out in 2013: *Pacific Walkers*, her sixth collection of poems (U. of Washington Press), and *Boneland*, her fourth book of linked stories (U. of Oklahoma Press). A Professor Emerita at E.W.U., she teaches in the low-residency MFA Program at Vermont College of Fine Arts. See more here: http://photoemsbynancevanwinckel.zenfolio.com/

**Shawn Vestal** is the author of *Godforsaken Idaho*, a collection of short stories. A columnist at *The Spokesman-Review* in Spokane, he also teaches in the Eastern Washington University MFA program.

**Jess Walter** is the author of eight books. He's been a #1 New York Times bestseller, a finalist for the 2006 National Book Award and the PEN/USA Literary prize in both fiction and nonfiction, and won the 2005 Edgar Allan Poe Award. His work has been published in 30 languages and his short fiction has appeared in *Best American Short Stories*, *Harpers*, *McSweeney's*, *Esquire* and elsewhere.

**Ellen Welcker** is a poet whose work can be found at ewelcker.tumblr.com. She coordinates the Bagley Wright Lecture Series on Poetry, works in the Writers' Center at EWU, and hosts SpoPo, a living room poetry reading series in Spokane.

# **Bios** continued

**Maya Jewell Zeller**'s poetry has won awards from *Sycamore Review*, *New South*, *New Ohio Review*, *Dogwood*, *Florida Review* and *Crab Orchard Review*. Her book, *Rust Fish*, was published by Lost Horse Press. She teaches English at Gonzaga University.